"Few culinary historians have written as lovingly and knowingly and, certainly, wittily as Will Weaver has on his favorite subject – the true offerings of the Pennsylvania Dutch kitchen. With Dutch Treats he puts fresh polish on the apple. It will be a treat, indeed, for the serious scholar as much as the adventurous home cook."

~ *Rick Nichols, former longtime food columnist for* The Philadelphia Inquirer

"Lavishly illustrated and culled from a lifetime of fieldwork in no less than twenty-five counties, *Dutch Treats* captures the wide diversity of Pennsylvania's folk culture of baking, and is a treasure trove of lesser-known recipes. Far from the contrived foodways of the Lancaster County tourist industry and beyond even the authentic local sources, which tend to be limited in their geographic range, Dr. Weaver delights with a broader spectrum of Pennsylvania's baking traditions than anyone previously thought possible."

~ *Patrick J. Donmoyer, Pennsylvania German Cultural Heritage Center, Kutztown University*

"With his passion, energy, and discoveries in both kitchen and garden, William Woys Weaver has transformed the field of food scholarship – in fact, he is a national treasure. In *Dutch Treats*, he offers the definitive guide to a little-understood American regional cuisine."

~ *Jane Lear, co-author of* One Spice, Two Spice

"Those warm, buttery treasures were like a secret we knew only in Pennsylvania. Dr. Weaver's latest book bridges our childhood and lifelong love of baked goods and sweets with the history and folklore that make enjoying them all the more soulful. These foods have already been shared across America, but here in *Dutch Treats* we get to appreciate and be proud of where they came from – and revel in the fact that we can continue to share them for time to come."

~ **Palmer Marinelli,** *Philadelphia chef and food activist*

"William Woys Weaver singlehandedly saved fish peppers, and he is the reason that semmels, rusks and clafty pudding are on the menu at Woodberry Kitchen. *Dutch Treats* continues the essential body of work that includes *Country Scrapple* and *Sauerkraut Yankees*, with an authoritative yet affectionate portrait of Pennsylvania Dutch baking, connecting us with the traditions, people and landscape of this special place. Like a warm shoofly cake, *Dutch Treats* is a gift that will continue to enrich the conversation and the table."

~ **Spike Gjerde,** *2015 James Beard Award for Best Chef: Mid-Atlantic*

"The name William Woys Weaver guarantees us original research into a freshly discovered subject. In *Dutch Treats* he explores his own home ground with one hundred cakes, cookies and puddings from the Pennsylvania Dutch country that hark back to European traditions – with tempting illustrations of recipes such as Peach Schnitz and Saffron Bread. Schluppers, anyone?"

~ **Anne Willan,** *culinary historian, writer, founder of École de Cuisine La Varenne*

DUTCH TREATS

DUTCH TREATS

Heirloom Recipes from Farmhouse Kitchens

William Woys Weaver

st. lynn's
press

PITTSBURGH

Dutch Treats
Heirloom Recipes from Farmhouse Kitchens

ISBN-13: 978-1-943366-04-0

Library of Congress Control Number: 2016938555
CIP information available upon request

First Edition, 2016

St. Lynn's Press . POB 18680 . Pittsburgh, PA 15236
412.381.9933 . www.stlynnspress.com

Book design – Holly Rosborough
Editor – Catherine Dees
Editorial Intern – Christina Gregory

Photo credits:
All photographs and food styling by William Woys Weaver unless otherwise noted.
Photo on page xiv, Dutch Butter Cake, Leopard Cake, Osterburg Easter Cake, Railroad Cake, Rough-and-Ready Cake, St. Gertrude's Day Datsch, Lebanon Rusk, and Potato Crumb Datsch are photos created by teamwork with Patrick Donmoyer and William Woys Weaver.
Author photo by Rob Cardillo.

Cover image: Bishop's Bread

Printed in China on certified FSC (Forest Stewardship Council) recycled paper using soy-based inks. This paper was sourced responsibly in a way that ensures the long-term health of forests.

This title and all of St. Lynn's Press books may be purchased for educational, business or sales promotional use. For information please write:
Special Markets Department . St. Lynn's Press . POB 18680 . Pittsburgh, PA 15236

10 9 8 7 6 5 4 3 2 1

For Cheryl Long, one of the most
special of all the Pennsylvania Dutch
I have been blessed to know.
Dutch Cousin, Guardian Angel,
Cheryl has always been my Rock.
Thank you for what you have done for me.
This book is your spiritual child.

Table of Contents

INTRODUCTION

DUTCH TREATS:

Cuisine as Living Tradition

*P*ennsylvania is one of the few places in the United States where rich folk tradition and the culinary arts meld seamlessly to create a magical yet down-to-earth regional cookery, unlike any other in the Old World or New. Pennsylvania Dutch cookery – the real thing, not the pallid tourist knock-off – remains a buried treasure in America's own back-yard: not yet trendy, but moving in that direction. The 25 counties that represent the broadest extent of the Pennsylvania Dutch Country form a Switzerland-size heartland of culinary tradition based on local produce, wild-foraged ingredients, and a respect for the living soil inherited from Old World farming customs. The iconic stone farmhouses of rural Pennsylvania have become lasting metaphors for all that is American in the best sense of cultural fusion and a food culture derived directly from the landscape that nurtures it.

The term Pennsylvania Dutch applies to all the many immigrant groups who came to this region from different parts of Germany and Switzerland. Many people mistakenly believe that Pennsylvania Dutch means Amish: it does not – the Amish represent about five percent of the total Pennsylvania Dutch population. The use of "Dutch" by colonial officials is an old English vernacular, which applied to anyone from the Rhine Valley: Low Dutch from Holland, High Dutch from Switzerland. Even William Shakespeare used this term, and not surprising, this is also the label the Dutch prefer themselves and for their language since their culture is no longer German. It quickly evolved into an American identity of its own, as the recipes in this book should demonstrate.

Calendula – the official flower of the Pennsylvania Dutch

While fieldwork has identified more than 1600 unique dishes not found in cookbooks or restaurants, I have culled from that list what I feel are the best from our baking tradition. This is the first book to explore traditional Pennsylvania Dutch baking, with about 100 representative recipes (I say "about 100" because some recipes contain other recipes within them so it's all in how one counts). Most of these recipes have never before been published. Indeed, most of them have been acquired only through fieldwork interviews and come with backstories – and often with folk tales as fresh and compelling as anything collected in the 1800s by the Brothers Grimm.

Our food traditions have their own saints and sinners, their own stories, and a cast of characters as colorful as the lush, bountiful landscape that has produced them. Where else in America will you find the *Waldmops*? He is considered "lord of the beasts," a father figure to all the forest creatures as well as king of the wee folk who protect our gardens and fields. Our Waldmops rules over fields and gardens and the "colors" of the four winds that define the year's growing seasons. The moon may instruct us when to plant, but it is the green wind from the southeast that bears the warm spring rains required for a garden over-plus and the harvest bounty that makes the recipes in this book possible.

You may spot our Waldmops cookie lurking along the margins of several pictures in this book. According to folklore, he wears a coat woven of willow leaves, spleenwort, and moss and dons a magical top hat fashioned from ivy, wintergreen and yew twigs – or from mistletoe when he can find it. Waldmops has a daughter called *Ringelros* (wreath rose) who is none other than the sunny calendula, the official flower of the Pennsylvania Dutch. She inhabits kitchen gardens to protect them and the farmhouse from plagues and pestilence, and thus figures in many recipes of a curative nature.

The Waldmops can also claim a bad-tempered brother known as the *Bucklich Mennli* (little humpback man) who inhabits dark places in houses and barns. He is the bane of the Pennsylvania Dutch kitchen due to his pranks: ruining cakes, upsetting rising bread or stealing cookies hot from the oven. The old custom was to appease him by setting out a saucer of cream and a piece of cake on the hearth to keep him from meddling in household affairs. If he rose too far out of line, it was always possible to invoke St. Gertrude to send in her cats, since the little humpback man was terrified they would eat him – and they probably would.

St. Gertrude was the patron saint of kitchen gardens and cats. Her official day was observed throughout the Dutch Country on March 17, the traditional start of spring planting for the Pennsylvania Dutch. Gertrude's Datsch (a type of hearth bread, page 103) was scattered in the four corners of kitchen gardens to insure that the wee folk who lived there would continue to guard and protect it for the benefit of the household that oversaw its planting. Gertrude and Ringelros worked together to make certain that the bees found their nectar and that coriander yielded enough seed for Christmas baking, and caraway for cakes and pretzels.

These characters, mythical or real depending on your closeness to Nature, stand behind the stories for many of the recipes in this book. They give our remarkable cuisine its meaning and connectedness to who we are as Pennsylvania Dutch and to our place in the Green World around us.

So it should come as no surprise that with so many spirits in the wheat and Ancient Goodness in the land, we have made a special effort in this cookbook to invoke only the best ingredients, Pennsylvania grown, since they represent our cultural authenticity as we know it – and perhaps are one reason many Pennsylvania Dutch are known to attain such a great and fruitful age. Thus, in every recipe we have used wherever possible locally raised, harvested and milled non-GMO organic flours and other local ingredients. Pennsylvania is the third most important agricultural state in the country, and the leading source of fresh produce on the East Coast. We represent a special niche in American cuisine. It may be no exaggeration to suggest that American Cookery was invented here (a tale of culinary fusionism that I intend to take up in a future book on Philadelphia cuisine).

For those unfamiliar with this aspect of American history, the fusion of different early immigrant cultures first arose in colonial Pennsylvania, a region where free-minded Quakers encouraged different peoples and religions to settle side by side, to intermarry and share the bounties of the Peaceable Kingdom together. While the Pennsylvania Dutch managed to retain their own distinctive identity, their culinary traditions were quickly Americanized, and that is why the recipes in this book represent a New World culinary tradition unique among all other American regional cookeries.

The roots of Pennsylvania Dutch cookery trace to Southwest Germany and Alsace in such foods as New Year's Pretzels, *Lebkuchen*, or Adam and Eve Cookies. But through the blending of Old World regionalisms and New World realities an entirely new culinary expression was born. Old Germany knows nothing of Fish Pie or Whoopie Cakes, Chinquapin Jumbles, Boskie Boys or Peanut Datsch. The inventiveness of the Pennsylvania Dutch housewife has taken these heirloom baking traditions into areas unknown to their Old World ancestors. The end result is cookery as thoroughly American as Shoofly Pie.

From a technical standpoint, Pennsylvania Dutch baking is highly developed and based on the idea

of interchangeable parts. This harks back to the innate frugality of the Dutch themselves, who waste nothing and find creative ways to repurpose leftover food. Thus, dough for one type of bread can be reinvented with additional ingredients to make something else. Crumbs from cakes can be used to dust bread or cake pans, crackers are turned into pie, pie crusts can be transformed into cookies or into the ever-pragmatic Slop Tarts that Dutch children find in their school lunch boxes.

Since there are many technical dialect terms in Pennsylvania Dutch cookery, I have included a glossary (page 163) illustrated with pictures of traditional baking tools and ingredients. You do not need to own these utensils to bake the Dutch way, but it helps to know what they look like so that you can find substitutes if you want them.

About the photography: Pennsylvania Dutch food, especially farmhouse cookery, has an appearance that is unique; it looks best straight from the oven in settings that represent the spirit of its long tradition. With that in mind – and with an eye long trained in the cuisine and the tonalities of the ever-changing seasons – I photographed many of the recipes at the historic Sharadin Farmstead, home of the Pennsylvania German Cultural Heritage Center at Kutztown University.

Pennsylvania Dutch cookery, whether savory meals or festive baking, is highly seasonal and pegged inevitably to the phases of the moon, as outlined in our old-time almanacs. These traditions are probably best expressed in the folk tales about our Waldmops, who represents the Earth in all its diversity and fertility. By leaving Antler Cookies for him in the woods each *Fastnacht* (Fat Tuesday), we remind him of our respect for the Green World around us and that we are friends and allies in making this land a better place.

While the Waldmops was certainly no baker, his protective supervision over the grains that produced the flours used in our baking tradition was considered vital to the outcome of every baking day. The so-called "spirits in the wheat" connected his natural world with that of the table.

The spirituality of Pennsylvania Dutch food, whether folk belief or religious, is doubtless best expressed by our bread, which is the subject of the first chapter.

Saffron Bread

ONE

FESTIVE BREADS

Fescht Brode

If we reduced Pennsylvania Dutch farmhouse culture to one iconic dish, it would be sauerkraut without a question; yet eye-catching, delicious-tasting breads also define the traditional Pennsylvania Dutch table, with their remarkable range of festive shapes and flavors. During the colonial period, Pennsylvania became the breadbasket of the English colonies. The main growers of that wheat were the Pennsylvania Dutch. They measured their wealth in bushels of wheat, they paid bills with it, and their bread baking was legendary. Any farmhouse worthy of the name possessed a beehive bake oven in the yard not far from the kitchen door. It was the weekly task of the mistress of the household to bake bread, pies and cakes – often on a massive scale. Baking was generally undertaken on Fridays so that there would be plenty to eat for Sunday dinner. However, when the holidays drew near or a wedding loomed on the calendar, the baking frenzy went into high gear, usually with

the help of relatives or friends from the neighborhood. The most traditional of these specialty items demanded their own shape, flavor and story. That is the subject of the chapter at hand.

The original Pennsylvania Dutch term for cake was *Siesser Brod* (sweetened bread), which in local parlance among the non-Dutch became "cake bread." *Siesser Brod* implied that the *Fordeeg* (foundation dough) was bread dough, the very same used for making common loaf bread, except that the foundation dough was then elaborated with any number of additional ingredients, such as eggs, honey, sugar, spices, saffron or dried fruit. These dressed-up breads took many forms, perhaps the oldest and most classic being *Schtrietzel*, which was a loaf of bread shaped like a braid, or as some culinary historians would suggest, a head of grain. Regardless of the symbolic meaning, these were special occasion foods and some were only made once a year. Many did not contain much honey or sugar since they were meant to be toasted and eaten with jam – the classic spread being Quince Honey *(Qwiddehunnich)* as presented on page 11. One of the basic recipes in this category, which became a fixture of many Sunday dinners, is so-called Dutch Bread, in some respects a study in simplicity because it is not very rich in terms of ingredients. Our heirloom recipe was preserved by Anna Bertolet Hunter (1869-1946) of Reading, Pennsylvania. The Bertolets are one of the oldest and most distinguished Pennsylvania Dutch families in Berks County and have always been at the forefront when it comes to preserving local culture.

Aside from farmhouse baking, there are period records from before the Civil War of bakeries in large towns that specialized in festive breads like the New Year's Pretzel, large gingerbread figures and *Hutzelbrodt* – since these breads require an oversized oven. In rural areas, this task sometimes fell to local taverns, which possessed the bake-oven capacity and turnover of customers to generate extra money from seasonal sales. It was also common for people in the neighborhood to pitch in to help the taverns during the busy holidays – and get paid with Christmas baked goods in return for the work.

One of the earliest historical recipes for *Siesser Brod* surfaced in the 1813 account book of Lebanon County furniture maker Peter Ranck (1770-1851), who must have acquired auxiliary training in baking. Ranck called his recipe *Zuckerweck* (sugar buns) because he shaped the bread into small rolls for Christmas or New Year's. In short, the same foundation dough was used to make Dutch Cake (Pennsylvania Dutch *Gugelhupf*), New Year's Boys, Lebanon Rusks and Christmas dinner rolls called "Kissing Buns" *(Kimmichweck).*

Gingerbread mold depicting New Year's Pretzel, Schtrietzel and Kissing Buns

The kissing buns acquired their name because they consisted of two round buns baked side-by-side so that they would "kiss" and stick together – they were sent to the table in pairs as shown in the old gingerbread mold above.

Plain bread rolls made in the same shape with the best sort of wheat flour were called wedding rolls because they were expensive and were only served on high occasions of that nature – of course the kissing bread was also symbolic of the wedding couple and the work cut out for them on their honeymoon. The earliest known Pennsylvania Dutch image of these kissing buns appeared in a carving on the 1745 case clock of Lancaster bread baker Andreas Beyerle. Thus, while the written record in cookbooks may be skimpy, other types of evidence attest to the important place such festive breads once held in traditional Pennsylvania Dutch culture. For this chapter, I have selected several iconic breads representing the major calendar events in the year.

Apple Bread or Schnitzing Bread
Ebbelbrod odder Schnitzerei Brod

This fulsome old-time recipe came to light in an 1856 Hagerstown almanac published in German for the Pennsylvania Dutch community living in western Maryland. Fall schnitzing parties were at one time a focal point of Pennsylvania Dutch country life. The abundance of apples in fall invited creative ways to use them. Mealy apples that were not fit for schnitzing were peeled and cooked down for apple sauce or apple butter. The cores and parings were boiled to make a "tea" that was also used in apple butter production or employed as part of the liquid starter for apple bread, one of the festive foods served when entire neighborhoods gathered in a local farm-house to pare and slice apples for drying. While many hands lightened the burden of work, flasks of apple jack and rye whiskey and romantic rendezvous in the haymow more or less defined the evening.

Apple Bread is also one of the basic doughs used to make Christmas *Hutzelbrod* (page 12). While definitely spectacular as toast liberally spread with apple butter and rich, fragrant, melting Amish Roll Butter, the delicate fruit flavor of apple bread also complements the wonderful array of dried fruits stuffed inside this holiday treat. As a variation to our recipe below, you can add chopped apple, peach

or pear Schnitz to the sponge right before adding the flour. If you want to try your hand at baking this bread the old way by proofing it in traditional rye straw baskets, refer to the special instructions in the sidebar.

Peach Schnitz

3 cups (750ml) lukewarm apple puree (or warm unsweetened apple sauce)
7 to 7½ cups (940g) bread flour
1 cup (250ml) apple "tea" (see note)
1 tablespoon (15g) sugar
½ ounce (15g) dry active yeast
1 tablespoon (15g) plus 1½ teaspoon salt

Milk Glaze:
1 tablespoon (15g) unsalted soft butter
1 tablespoon (15ml) whole milk

Combine 3 cups (750ml) lukewarm apple puree with 3 cups (375g) bread flour and 1 tablespoon (15g) salt. Proof the yeast in the lukewarm apple water sweetened with 1 tablespoon (15g) sugar. Once the yeast is foaming vigorously, add it to the apple sponge. Cover and set away in a warm place until double in bulk and forming bubbles on the surface. Then stir down, add the remaining 1½ teaspoon of salt and approximately 4½ cups (565g) of the remaining bread flour and chopped dried fruit (optional). Use only enough flour to keep the dough from sticking to the fingers. Knead 5 to 10 minutes or until the dough becomes soft and spongy.

Divide the dough into two equal portions. Knead these again and shape into loaves. Place the loaves in two well-greased bread pans and cover (traditional loaves were raised in round rye straw baskets and turned out to bake, like French boules – see photo opposite and sidebar instructions). Set aside and let the bread raise above the tops of the bread pans or baskets, the higher the better. Preheat the oven to 450F (235C). Bake the bread at this temperature for 15 minutes, then reduce the heat to 400F (205C) and bake for another 15 minutes. Then reduce the temperature to 375F (190C) and bake for 25 to 30 minutes or until the bread taps hollow on the bottom. As soon as the bread comes from the oven, remove it from the pans, combine the soft butter and milk until creamy, then brush the crust (in former times this was done with a piece of flannel or a goose feather). Otherwise, brush

the crust with cold apple water or with cold applejack. Let the bread cool before slicing.

Note: The tea is made by boiling the cores and skins for about 30 minutes. Clear, unsweetened apple juice may be used as a substitute.

Special Instructions for Baking in Rye Straw Baskets

Traditional Pennsylvania Dutch farmhouse bread was proofed in rye straw baskets which gave the loaves their distinctive round shape and basket pattern in the crust. Rye straw baskets are still available from several basket makers in the region. To use them the old way, dust the interiors liberally with GMO-free roasted cornmeal, then place a large ball of dough in each basket (we used one large basket for the photograph). Cover the basket and set it in a warm place. When the dough has risen above the top of the basket, turn it out onto a baking sheet or pizza tin, let it recover for about 15 minutes and then bake as instructed in the recipe. Do not brush the bread with the creamed butter mixture or cold apple water if you want the loaf to retain its rustic dusted-with-flour appearance. Otherwise, while the bread is still hot from the oven, quickly brush off the cornmeal and apply the basting mixture as directed.

Apple Bread (Schmitzing Bread)

Baked Anise Dumplings for Festive Occasions
Backgnepp fer Feschtdaage

During the holidays years ago these dumplings were fairly common in Pennsylvania Dutch bakeries and farm markets, where they were sold under the local name *fresh rusk*. The dumplings do make excellent rusks because they dry out after a day or two, which is why they are best fresh from the oven. The unused dumplings were usually recycled in some manner, often sliced and baked in puddings or in a fruit *Schlupper* (see chapter xx). These particular dumplings are not extremely sweet because they were intended to be eaten with sauce or stewed fruit – such as peaches stewed with dried sour cherries, or currants when in season. In fact, the beaten egg and sugar topping can be omitted because the dumplings are just as good plain. This same basic dough recipe also can be used for making a braided *Aniskranz* (anise-flavored wreath bread) or it can be baked in a Bundt mold. Excellent when served with tea or coffee or with sweet wine.

Yield: Approximately 20 Servings

½ cup (125ml) whole milk
¼ ounce (7g) yeast
6 ounces (185g) unsalted butter
4 ounces (125g) sugar
4 large eggs
6¼ cups (815g) bread flour
2 teaspoons ground coriander
1½ teaspoons ground cardamom
Grated zest of 1 lemon
1 tablespoon anise seeds (or more to taste)

Topping:
1 beaten egg white
1 tablespoon (15g) vanilla sugar
1 tablespoon sliced almonds or chopped
   hickory nuts

Scald the milk and cool to lukewarm. Proof the yeast in it. Cream the butter and sugar and set aside. In a separate bowl, beat the eggs until lemon color, then combine with the proofed yeast. Add this to the reserved butter-and-sugar mixture. Sift together the flour and spices, then gradually sift in the flour to form soft dough; use only enough flour as necessary to keep the dough from sticking to the fingers. Knead 10 minutes, then cover and let the dough rise in a warm place until double in bulk. Knock down and roll out in a rectangle ½ inch (1.25cm) thick. Scatter the anise seed and grated lemon over this, then fold the dough over twice and knead well until pliant. Form into 20 2-ounce (60g) balls and set them in a buttered *Schales* pan (see glossary, page 163) or in a shallow cake tin of similar proportions to rise in a warm place. Or roll into a wreath or circle and cover. Let the dough recover for 25 minutes. Brush with an egg white beaten until forming stiff peaks and scatter liberally with vanilla sugar and almonds (optional). Bake for 25 to 30 minutes in an oven preheated to 375F (190C). Or bake in a Bundt mold well greased and dusted with bread or cake crumbs for the same period of time. It should tap hollow when done.

Bean Day Bread
Buhnedaag Brod

Depending on which farmer you ask, *Buhnedaag* (Bean Day) is either June 4 or June 5 (St. Boniface Day). This is the critical date on the Pennsylvania Dutch garden calendar by which time most pole beans and lima beans should be in the ground if they are to produce seed for the next season. This is also the date when kitchen gardeners should start planting bush beans in 2-week successions so that there will be a fresh crop right up until frost. With so much hinging on this important date, we would have thought that some entrepreneurial Dutchman would have come up with a Bean Planting Festival, but the truth of the matter is, at that time of year everyone in the Dutch Country is too busy in the garden to bother with such distractions.

Just the same, Bean Day has its advocates, not to mention its unofficial herb: *Buhnegreidel* ("bean plant"), otherwise known as summer savory. Eating beans with summer savory is an old-time preventive remedy for gas (you know the kind we mean), so it is not surprising that it also figures in Bean Day Bread. That said, some cooks prefer to add sage (or a combination of sage and savory), while others add calendula petals for good luck, calendulas being the Dutch national flower. No one knows exactly when Bean Day was first observed, although we suspect it existed in many tentative and perhaps purely pragmatic forms until the 1840s, when Pennsylvania Dutch soldiers brought back black beans from the Mexican War.

Mexican Black Turtle Beans were suddenly touted as the next best thing to turtle soup (only if you add enough Madeira!), and while black beans were not exactly a Pennsylvania Dutch ideal – they preferred white, brown or speckled varieties, since bread made with black beans looks like rye bread – thus a good idea was born. I have taken it a little further by adding garlic and sunflower seeds. I have baked the loaf shown in the picture in a traditional square bride cake tin. More on bride cake tins on page 18. Otherwise, this recipe will make two loaves when baked in bread pans.

Yield: 2 loaves

1⅓ cups (8 ounces/250g) black beans
1½ tablespoons grated unsweetened baking
  chocolate
1 cup (250ml) strong black coffee
½ ounce (15g) dry active yeast
1 cup (250ml) lukewarm milk or potato water
2 tablespoons (30ml) walnut oil or vegetable oil
5 cups (625g) bread flour (more or less)
1½ teaspoons minced garlic
1½ tablespoons salt
4 tablespoons (50g) toasted sunflower seeds
2 tablespoons (5g) fresh summer savory leaves, or
  1½ tablespoons dry thyme leaves

Cook the beans in 1½ cups (375ml) water until tender. Then puree the beans with the cooking liquid. Put this in a deep work bowl. Grate the chocolate, then dissolve it in the hot coffee. Add this to the bean puree. Proof the yeast in lukewarm milk or potato water. Once the yeast is actively foaming, add it to the bean mixture. Whisk to create a smooth batter, add the oil, then sift in 3 cups (375g) of flour. Cover with a damp cloth and let the sponge rise until double in bulk.

Once risen and developing bubbles on top, stir down and add the garlic, salt, sunflower seeds, savory and about 2 cups (250g) of flour – only enough so that when kneaded, the dough no longer adheres to the hands. It is important to keep the dough as soft and pliant as possible. Knead for about 5 minutes, dusting the hands with flour, then cover and let the dough rise again until about double in bulk.

Knock down, form into loaves and lay them in greased bread pans measuring 4 by 11 inches (10 by 28 cm). Cover again. Once the dough has recovered and risen to within 1 inch (2.5cm) of the top of the loaf pans, set the bread in the middle of the oven, pre-heated to 450F (230C) Bake 15 minutes, then reduce heat to 400F (200C). Bake another 15 minutes, then reduce heat to 350F (180C) and continue to bake for 30 to 35 minutes or until the bread taps done. Brush with ice water as soon as the bread comes from the oven. Cool on racks.

Butter Semmels
Budder Semmle

There is no precise English word for *Semmel*. The German word derives from Latin *similia* which originally meant the finest grade of wheat flour. Today Semmel applies mostly to fine dinner rolls or to dainty breads made from the best sort of wheat. Those rolls are the equivalent to what the medieval English called manchets; the inner crumbs of these rolls are still prized as something superior to common bread crumbs. The crumbs are even sold commercially in Germany under the name *Semmelmehl*. However, dinner rolls in Pennsylvania Dutch are called *Weck*, so there is no ambiguity as to what is meant by Butter Semmels: they are miniature envelopes designed to hold a host of fillings and thus closely resemble Jewish *Hamantaschen* made at Purim. The two are probably related through a common medieval ancestor.

In her narrative cookbook *Mary at the Farm* (1916), author Edith Thomas was meticulous in including a recipe for Butter Semmels, knowing as she did how important they were in Pennsylvania Dutch cuisine. She obtained her working recipe from her Quaker friend Mary Lippincott, whose husband was part owner of an iron foundry in Lehigh County. This little bit of recipe sleuthing revealed two important points about Butter Semmels: they were definitely a feature of upper class Pennsylvania Dutch entertaining and they were especially popular among the Moravians as one of several foods served during the holiday season, when they threw open their homes to display *Putz*, elaborately constructed scenes depicting the Christmas story.

We shall pass over the Butter Semmels filled with duck liver or minced smoked pheasant and concentrate on the species made for dessert. They can be filled with little scoops of ground nuts and sugar, almond paste, dried fruit or jam. I have left them plain, although Quince Honey (see opposite page) or raspberry jam flavored with rosewater can turn these happy pastries into true food memories.

Butter Semmels

Yield: 5 to 6 dozen

½ ounce (15g) dry active yeast
1 cup (250ml) lukewarm potato water (98F/37C)
¾ cup (185g) unsalted butter and lard (half and half), or all butter
2 cups (400g) warm mashed potatoes
1 cup (175g) light brown sugar
1 tablespoon (15g) salt
2 large eggs
7 cups (875g) organic bread flour
Melted unsalted butter
Superfine sugar

Proof the yeast in the potato water. While the yeast is proofing, whip the butter and lard into the warm mashed potatoes. Then add the sugar and salt. Once the potatoes are tepid, beat the eggs until lemon-color and frothy, and fold them into the potato mixture. Add the proofed yeast, then sift in 2 cups (250g) of flour.

Work this into soft dough, cover and let it double in bulk (about 5 hours). Then gradually sift in the remaining flour, only enough to make the dough stiff so that it does not stick to the hands. Knead well until it becomes soft and tacky.

Flour your work surface and rolling pin, then roll out pieces of dough into sheets ½ inch (1.25cm) thick. Cut the dough into 2-inch (5cm) squares. Take the corners of each square and fold them toward the center, envelope fashion. Pinch the tips together tightly – otherwise, they will pop open when during baking. Dot the pinch with butter and pinch again. Set the Semmels on greased baking sheets to recover.

Preheat the oven to 350F (180C). Once the dough has risen, bake in the preheated oven for 15 to 20 minutes – 18 minutes seems to be a reliable average. Remove from the oven, and while still hot, brush the Semmels with melted butter and then dust them with superfine sugar (caster sugar) or a mix of sugar and cinnamon.

Note: This same dough can be used for making *Fastnachts* (page 69), decorative New Year's Pretzels (page 22), and New Year's Boys (page 21). Butter Semmels were also made for Valentine's parties, but instead of a fruit or jam filling, motto papers were placed inside. Motto papers are like the little sayings placed inside Chinese fortune cookies, except that the theme of the mottos always dealt with love or romance.

Quince Honey
Quiddehunnich

Anyone who undertakes a cursory glance through the cookbooks printed in nineteenth-century Pennsylvania soon realizes that quince honey stands out as a common culinary theme, whether the book was published in Erie, Meadville, Greensburg, Lancaster or Easton. Through state fairs and multitudes of blue ribbons, the Pennsylvania Dutch love of quince honey spread all across Pennsylvania regardless of cultural boundaries; every fundraising cookbook before 1920 with a church connection seems to feature at least one version of this classic regional confection.

For the record, quince honey is not literally honey and making it is not as simple as following a recipe for jam because the success of the endeavor hangs, not surprisingly, on the condition of the fresh fruit. Classic quince honey is quince jam (quince cooked in sugar) reduced to a smooth spread with a flavor that cannot be described easily because you must begin with tree-ripe fruit. You will know they are ripe if you can smell their perfume, which will fill an entire room with the fragrance of sweet peas, vanilla and orchids. It is that ethereal quality that must be captured in the jam. So, in order to make this recipe worthwhile, select at market only those quince that remind you of perfume. You can make quince water by boiling the cores and skins 30 minutes in spring water until gray and slimy. You can then use this "tea" as pectin for other preserve recipes. Meanwhile, I have tested quince honey several times and suggest making it this way (see note below):

Yield: 8½ cups (2¼ liters)

2 pounds (1 kg) cooked pureed quince
2 cups (500ml) quince water (see note below)
¼ cup (65ml) fresh lemon juice
1 box Sure-Jell
5½ cups (1.375kg) sugar

Put the pureed quince, quince water, lemon juice and Sure-Jell in a deep preserving pan and bring to a full boil over a high heat. Add the sugar. Bring to a rolling boil and boil for one minute. Remove from the heat and transfer to hot sanitized jars.

Note: While I do not prefer Sure-Jell because of the overabundance of sugar it requires, nonetheless, the recipe will work as directed and it will not disappoint. I suggest doing it this way first, then once perfected, you may want to explore other pectin sources. That said, this jam will jell without Sure-Jell as long as you use the pectin tea, but cooking time will depend on the state of the fruit, a thing we cannot measure or predict in printed recipes, although 20 minutes of steady boiling should do it.

Christmas Fruit Loaf
Hutzelbrod

Hutzelbrod is one of the forgotten culinary classics of the Dutch Country. The name derives from *Hutzle*, a term for dried fruit but especially for dried plums or pears, one of the main ingredients. There was a time when you could find these wonderful fruit-filled breads in nearly every county town during the holiday season. Today, only a few families still make them. Part of the reason is that they require advance planning and two days of preparation.

The earliest recorded Pennsylvania Dutch recipe for this Christmas treat appeared in *Der Amerikanische Bauer* [The American Farmer], a Harrisburg farm journal published in the 1850s. It is unusual to find any sort of recipes for *Hutzelbrod*, because the ingredients were quite variable and the bread part could consist of a wide variety of doughs, although basic sourdough bread was the predominant choice. In general, since the commercial loaves were large, often measuring 40 inches (100cm) in length, *Hutzelbrod* was considered a baker's showpiece, much like New Year's pretzels – not to mention that bakeries owned ovens large enough to accommodate breads that size. In farmhouse cookery, the loaves were prepared somewhat smaller, ranging from 12 to 20 inches (30cm to 50cm). The 1850s recipe I consulted did not provide suggestions for dough other than bread dough, but it was absolutely clear about the filling. For the dough, I suggest using yeast-raised butter crust (page 112) because it is easy to handle and bakes a beautiful golden color. If you choose to use the apple bread recipe (page 3), cut the quantity in half and start the dough the night before, since it takes longer to rise.

Yield: One 20-inch (50cm) loaf, or
two 10-inch (25cm) loaves

½ **cup (50g) dried pears, chopped into pea-size pieces**
½ **cup (40g) apple schnitz, chopped into pea-size pieces**
¼ **cup (50g) candied citron, chopped**
¼ **cup (50g) whole golden raisins**
⅓ **cup (35g) slivered almonds**
½ **cup (125g) sugar**
½ **cup (125g) apple jack or pear brandy**
1 batch yeast-raised butter crust (page 112)
Honey crumbs (see sidebar)

Topping:
1 egg yolk
1 tablespoon (30ml) milk
Candied angelica as decoration after baking

The day before you plan to bake, combine the chopped dried fruit, citron, raisins, almonds, sugar and wine. Cover and set aside to marinate 24 hours. The next day, drain the fruit mixture of all excess liquid and set aside. The excess liquid can be added to mincemeat pies or used as basting liquid for your Christmas turkey or goose.

Prepare the yeast-raised butter crust according to the directions on page 112. Cover and let the dough proof until double in bulk.

While the dough is proofing, make the honey crumbs as directed in the sidebar.

Once the dough has doubled in bulk, knock down and roll out in a rectangle 12 inches (30cm) wide and 20 inches (50cm) long. Trim off irregular edges for use

as ornamentation. Spread the drained, reserved fruit mixture over the rectangle of dough, then scatter the crumbs evenly over this. Roll up as tightly as possible, taking care to fold under the ends and pinch the seams closed. Ornament the loaf with strips of dough reserved for that purpose and little rings for the candied angelica (refer to the photograph). Set the bread on a large greased baking sheet, preferably one with raised sides in case the loaf leaks liquid from the fruit during baking (this saves cleaning the oven).

Cover and set aside in a warm place to rise (at least 40 minutes). While the bread is recovering, preheat the oven to 375F (190C). Brush the loaf with a mixture of 1 egg yolk and 1 tablespoon (15ml) of milk. Bake in the preheated oven for 35 to 40 minutes or until the bread taps hollow. Once the bread is cool, insert pieces of candied angelica in the small rings ornamenting the top.

Honey Crumbs

½ **cup (125g) sugar**
2 tablespoons (30g) cold, unsalted butter
¼ **cup (65ml) honey**
½ **cup (125g) flour**
1 tablespoon (5g) ground cardamom
1 teaspoon ground star anise
1 teaspoon anise seed (optional)

Using two forks or a pastry cutter, rub the ingredients together in a work bowl to form large, coarse crumbs. Do not handle. Keep the crumbs cool until needed. Use a spoon to scatter the crumbs over the fruit as directed in the recipe.

Cinnamon Rolls or "Snails"
Schnecke

These simple breakfast rolls are sometimes called cinnamon buns but they are not the same thing as Philadelphia sticky buns; rather, they are coils of slightly crisp-crusted "snails" perfect for that morning wake-up call or afternoon coffee break. Our recipe has been adapted from the original of Lancaster Mennonite Della C. Diffenbaugh (1875-1948). It is plain, the way Mennonites make the rolls, and thankfully not overly sweet. For a change of pace, use the poppy seed filling for the Easter Cake on page 47. The amount given for that cake will also make enough to fill these rolls, and the Pennsylvania Dutch name then changes to *Mohnschnecke* (poppy seed snails).

Yield: 18 to 20 rolls

2 tablespoons (30g) unsalted butter
2 tablespoons (30g) sugar
¼ teaspoon salt
1 cup (250ml) hot milk
½ oz. (15g) dry active yeast
½ cup (125ml) lukewarm milk (98F/37C)
2 large eggs
5 cups (625g) bread flour
2 tablespoons ground cinnamon
2 oz. (65g) soft unsalted butter
4 oz. (125g) brown sugar

Dissolve the butter, sugar and salt in the hot milk. Proof the yeast in the lukewarm milk. In a separate work bowl, beat the eggs until lemon color and frothy. When the hot milk is tepid, beat it into the eggs, then add the proofed yeast. Sift in 2½ cups (315g) of flour and work into a soft sponge. Cover and set aside to rise in a warm place until double in bulk.

Once the dough had doubled in bulk, work in the remaining flour and knead until soft and spongy. Roll out the dough on a clean work surface to form a large rectangle ½ inch (1.25cm) thick. Make a paste by creaming together the cinnamon, soft butter and brown sugar, then spreading this evenly over the dough. Starting on the long side of the rectangle, roll up the dough to create a long coil; slice the roll into 1-inch thick (2.5cm) pieces. Lay the slices slice side down in greased baking tins so that they barely touch. Cover and let the dough rise for about 30 minutes or until puffy.

Preheat the oven to 350F (180C) and bake the rolls for 25 minutes. Cool on racks and serve with strong black coffee.

Dutch Bread or Light Cake

Deitscher Brod odder G'gangene Kuche

This iconic Pennsylvania Dutch recipe was preserved by Anna Bertolet Hunter (1869-1946) of Reading. Mrs. Hunter and her son, Wellington, were deeply involved in organizing the Bertolet Family Association; she more or less took charge of the women's committee, which handled the refreshments for the various reunions. Her heirloom Dutch Bread was first served at a reunion held at Mineral Springs Park in Reading on August 5, 1900 and at many Bertolet family events thereafter. Like the Gerhart's Reunion Cake on page 42, Pennsylvania Dutch heritage was thus verified through the medium of food.

Recommended utensils: two 8 to 9 inch (20 to 23cm) cake tins at least 2 ½ inches (6 cm) deep.

Yield: Approximately 20 to 30 servings

Crumb Topping:
½ cup (60g) pastry flour
3 tablespoons (45g) cold unsalted butter
3 tablespoons (45g) sugar

Bread Ingredients:
8 tablespoons (125g) unsalted butter
¾ cup (185g) sugar
½ teaspoon salt
½ cup (100g) mashed potatoes
1 cup (250ml) whole milk
1½ teaspoons (about 15g) dry active yeast
1 cup (250ml) lukewarm milk or potato water
2 large eggs
4 to 5 cups (500g to 625g) bread flour

Before starting the bread, make the crumb topping by rubbing together the flour, butter and sugar until they form evenly sized crumbs. Set aside.

Put the butter, sugar, salt and mashed potatoes in a deep work bowl. Scald the milk and pour it boiling hot over these ingredients. Whisk until the mixture is smooth and all the sugar is dissolved. While this is cooling, proof the yeast in the lukewarm milk or potato water. Once it is foaming vigorously, combine with the milk mixture. Beat the eggs until frothy and lemon color, then add them to the liquid ingredients.

Sift the flour into the liquid mixture one cup at a time, stirring as you sift, until thick, sticky dough is formed. Cover and set aside in a warm place to triple in bulk.

Stir down with a spoon. Grease the cake pans and dust with bread crumbs. Divide the dough into two equal parts and spoon or ladle it into the cake pans. Sprinkle the prepared crumbs over the top. Set aside in a warm place until the dough rises to the top of the cake tin. While the dough is recovering, preheat the oven to 350F (180C). Once the dough has reached a height of no less than 2½ inches (6 cm), bake in the preheated oven for 40 to 45 minutes or until the breads tap done in the center. Cool on racks before removing from the baking tins. Do not slice while hot. Serve at room temperature.

Watch Point: If the dough is not allowed to triple in bulk in the first rising and double in bulk in the second, it will not bake properly and the centers will fall when taken from the oven. The first and second risings may require as long as 2 hours or more, depending on the temperature of your kitchen.

Easter Lamb
Oschter Lammbrod

Lamb-shaped breads baked specifically for Easter
have long been popular in the Dutch Country. They
were often placed in a basket surrounded by elaborately decorated Easter eggs near the altar in churches
or featured as the centerpiece of Easter displays in
bakeshop windows. Some of the oldest surviving
earthenware bread molds from the 1700s are devoted
to Easter Lambs and today they are greatly prized by
collectors and museums. The general custom was
to use any one of the yeast-raised doughs that also
stood service for Christmas or New Year's specialties. Thus, there was no particular traditional recipe

associated with Easter Lambs; you used whatever
sweetened bread recipe was part of your own family
tradition. On that point, six recipes in this chapter
can be used successfully to make an Easter Lamb:
Apple Bread, Baked Anise Dumplings, Lebanon
Rusk, New Year's Boys and New Year's Pretzel. The
Dutch Cake recipe in the cake chapter will also work
perfectly, since it takes easily to elaborate shapes.
Full batches of these recipes will make two or three
lambs, or even more, depending on the size of your
molds. For certain, you cannot make an Easter Lamb
without a mold, so a few words about what sort of
mold to use.

Aside from recent aluminum and glass copies, the
most popular molds today are the now-heirloom cast
iron lamb molds formerly made by the Griswold
Manufacturing Company (1865-1957) of Erie, Pennsylvania. These molds are commonly listed for sale
on eBay or stocked at antiques malls, and if they
are authentic will bear the manufacturer's number
866. Griswold molds are sturdy and were cast from
high quality Minnesota iron. They will produce
lambs about 10 inches (25cm) long. The firm also
published a pamphlet recipe for making a lamb
with their mold, but it is not a traditional Pennsylvania Dutch recipe. In fact, Griswold instructed its
users to cover the lamb with shredded coconut to
resemble wool. Pennsylvania Dutch Easter lambs
were considered bread, so they were rarely decorated
or iced. And since the lamb was a symbol of Christ,
this bread was treated with a certain amount of
religious reverence.

Baking a lamb in an antique earthenware mold
like the one in the illustration is not recommended.
These valuable and irreplaceable molds crack easily
(no steam vents), and if the dough expands too

much the mold will separate during baking and create a seam line all the way around the lamb; this is unsightly and must be trimmed off with sharp scissors right after the lamb comes from the oven. Reproduction earthenware molds are attractive but invite a similar problem, and in any case they must first be seasoned by boiling in water for about 50 minutes with two or three squeezed lemons – the more lemons the better. The acid tempers the glaze and clay body to help prevent cracking. Repeated use of a mold is the only way to learn exactly how much dough is required to fill the mold perfectly during baking. I recommend making your first few trials with plain bread dough. Weigh the amount of dough that was successful and file that figure with your recipe so that there is no guesswork the next time you bake. Also, be certain that there is ample dough in the area around the head; this is often the part of the lamb that causes the most problems for beginners.

Cast iron molds are better than other materials because they are heavy and can be sealed shut with metal clamps, thus assuring that no dough escapes. Iron molds must also be seasoned and that is done exactly like seasoning an iron skillet. The Griswold molds also have handles on both ends; this makes moving the mold in and out of the oven much easier – butter from the enriched bread dough can make the molds slippery, especially the glazed earthenware ones.

Whichever dough you use, it should be given its final proofing in a mold previously greased and dusted with flour. Baking is done while the mold is on its side, one half serving as a "lid." The baking temperature and time will be approximately the same as those given for each of the seven recommended doughs in their respective recipes, provided you position the mold on a middle rack in your oven. Keep in mind that cast iron tends to bake hot, so you may want to check on the lamb 10 minutes before it is done. Once fully baked, remove the lamb from the mold and cool it on a rack. It can be stored or frozen like common bread.

Lebanon Rusks or Potato Rusks
Libanon Siesse Weck
odder Gumbiere Rosk

Throughout the greater Delaware Valley there are two traditional types of rusk: the dry twice-baked rusk or *Zwieback* and the so-called "fresh" rusk, which is not baked a second time, and which is treated as a tea cake or something special to be eaten with coffee. It was either sliced and toasted or crumbled into the coffee to make "coffee soup." This latter type was quite popular among the Quakers, who may have contributed to its wide dissemination. The dough is similar (if not exactly the same) as the foundation dough used to make Philadelphia-style sticky buns. After baking the crumb is extremely light and will dry out easily, which is one reason the Dutch liked to add potatoes (this extended shelf life).

There were also two distinctly different ways of baking rusks: professional bakeries preferred to prepare them in tall, square tins called bride cake pans, which resulted in rusks at least 4 inches (10cm) in height. This is the type of rusk sold by Harrisburg baker Henry Becker in 1852 under the name Lebanon Rusk, one of the earliest known references to the term. Bakeries like Becker's probably favored this tin because bride cakes (a type of fruit cake), square loaves of bread, buns, and of course rusks, could be baked in them, thus reducing the need to invest in an array of specialized utensils. I have chosen this route in the baking instructions below, but you can also follow what was known as the "farmhouse style" by baking the rusks in shallow rusk pans like the one in the picture. This pan was common in farmhouse cookery because it was merely an adaptive reuse of a rectangular dripping pan. Indeed, rusk pans and dripping pans were functionally interchangeable.

Regardless of shape the most famous Pennsylvania Dutch fresh rusks are called Lebanon Rusks, mainly because they were popularized by Church of the Brethren women from Lebanon County via *The Inglenook*, their widely read household magazine. Just the same, there is no evidence that potato rusks (like "Lebanon" bologna) were actually invented in Lebanon. In fact, our recipe traces to Lizzie S. Risser (1880-1950) of Elizabethtown, in Lancaster County.

¼ ounce (7.5g) dry active yeast
1 cup (250ml) lukewarm potato water (98F/37C)
1 cup (200g) warm mashed potatoes
4 ounces (125g) unsalted butter
1 cup (250g) superfine sugar (also called caster
   sugar)
3 large eggs
5½ cups (690g) bread flour
1 egg white
Vanilla sugar

Proof the yeast in the potato water. Once the yeast is foaming vigorously, combine this with the mashed potatoes and whip smooth. Cream the butter and sugar. In a separate bowl, beat the eggs until lemon color and frothy, then combine with the creamed butter and sugar. Add this to the mashed potatoes and beat vigorously. Gradually sift in 4 cups (500g) of flour and work the batter into soft, sticky dough. Cover and allow to double in bulk in a warm place (1 ½ to 2 ½ hours, depending on the weather). Knock down and gently knead in the remaining 1 ½ cups (190g) of flour.

Butter the hands and mold out 30 balls of dough, each weighing 2 ounces (60g). Place the balls close together and evenly spaced in two greased spring-form cake pans without center tubes – the dough balls must "kiss" in all directions. Keep in mind that when baked in cake tins rusks rise up very high, so the pans must be at least 4 inches (10cm) deep; otherwise, the dough will overflow. Cover and allow the dough to rise again until over double in bulk (roughly 1 hour or more) or until the rusks reach the rim of the cake tin or rusk pan (if you are using one).

Preheat the oven to 350F (180C). Beat the egg white until stiff and forming peaks, then brush it over the surface of the rusks. Sprinkle with vanilla sugar (or lacking that, granulated sugar). Then bake in the pre-heated oven for 25 to 30 minutes, if you prefer a dark crust. If you prefer a lighter crust, preheat the oven to 325F (165C) and bake for 30 to 35 minutes. Once the rusks are done and tap hollow, remove from the oven and cake tins and cool on racks. Sprinkle again with sugar "to fill the valleys with snow," as an old cook once told me. Best when served the same day they are baked.

The Traditional Rusk Pan

Fresh rusks, *Schnecken* – even Philadelphia Sticky Buns – were commonly baked in a specific type of pan called a rusk pan. The standard dimensions were 7½ by 16½ by 2 inches (19 by 41 by 5 cm). The best sorts were made of heavy gauge Russia iron, an imported metal with a blu-ish-gray tinge on the surface. Antique rusk pans are now extremely rare, because once their usefulness as baking utensils passed, they could be sold for good money as scrap metal. The rusks in the photograph on the previous page have been baked in a traditional pan dating from the 1860s.

New Year's "Boys"
Neijohrsbuwe

Just as Christmas had its *Mummeli* (breads shaped like little men), New Year's featured its own special bread made from similar dough (or you can use the dough for Butter Semmels, page 9). These distinctive rolls or buns were produced mostly by small-town bakers for Silvester Night Balls (December 31st) held in local hotels and taverns, and one of them always contained a lucky coin. A huge eight-foot deep brick bake oven for making just such large-batch pastries survived well into the 1960s at the historic 1840s Quentin House Hotel in Quentin, near Lebanon, Pennsylvania.

We know from the field work of late Pennsylvania Dutch folklorist Alfred L. Shoemaker that due to their connection with Silvester Night (New Year's Eve), the rolls were also called Silvester Buns *(Silvesterweck)*, although the rural Dutch seem to have preferred the more euphemistic *Neijohrsbuwe* (New Year's Boys) in reference to the fact that the rolls have knobs or "heads" on the opposite ends, one for the old year and one for the new. This two-headed design appears to be traditional; however, the manner in which the rolls were decorated was a matter of personal fancy: some people preferred the so-called "two-headed fish" design shown in the picture. Others braided them to resemble heads of wheat or ornamented them with stars, swirling hex signs, or three X's. Dr. Shoemaker also discovered that New Year's Boys were given out to Belschnicklers when they went mumming house to house on Second Christmas (December 26). Otherwise, cookies and sweet pretzels were distributed instead like the orange pretzels on page 75.

Our original recipe comes from Fannie Coble (1870-1954) of Elizabethtown in Lancaster County. If you have leftover *Neijohrsbuwe* you can always slice them, dip them in beaten eggs and cook like French toast.

Yield: Six 7-inch (18cm) "Boys"

1 cup (225g) warm mashed potatoes
1 cup (250g) light brown sugar
2 teaspoons salt
½ ounce (15g) dry active yeast
1 cup lukewarm potato water or milk
6 tablespoons (90g) melted butter
2 large eggs
5 cups (625g) bread flour
1 egg yolk
2 tablespoons (30ml) milk

Beat the mashed potatoes and sugar together to form a smooth batter. Add the salt and set aside. Proof the yeast in the potato water or milk, and once it is foaming vigorously, add it to the mashed potato mixture. Then sift in 1½ cups (190g) of flour to make a sponge. Cover and set in a warm place to double in bulk. Once double in bulk, stir down and add the melted butter. Beat the eggs until lemon color and frothy and add them to the sponge. Gradually sift in the remaining flour one cup at a time, kneading as you add until a soft spongy dough forms that no longer sticks to the fingers.

Divide the dough into 6 equal pieces and shape each piece to form a small oblong roll with knobs or "heads" on each end (see picture). Using sharp scissors or a knife, cut three X marks on the body of each roll (or create a design of your own), and set them on a greased baking sheet to rise. Cover with a cloth and let the rolls recover for about 20 to 25 minutes. While they are rising, preheat the oven to 375F (190C). Before putting the rolls in the oven, make a wash with one egg yolk and 2 tablespoons (30ml) of milk. Take a soft brush and paint each loaf with this mixture. Bake in the preheated oven for approximately 35 minutes or until they tap done. Cool on racks.

New Year's Pretzel
(Neijohrsbrezel)

The pretzel is imbued with a great deal of colorful folklore in Pennsylvania Dutch culture, not surprising given the pretzel's ancient origins. When there was fog on the Blue Hills of Pennsylvania, parents used to tell their children that rabbits were baking pretzels in the woods; the fog was the smoke from their tiny ovens. Pretzels made from the flour of freshly harvested grain were called "rabbit pretzels," since the rabbit was a euphemism for spirits in the wheat, especially from the last sheaf of wheat taken from the field. The list of similar beliefs is long

and fascinating, which is perhaps why pretzels were thought to bring good luck (touched by the rabbit's paw?) and to make excellent gifts for important turning points on the calendar.

For this reason, very large and highly ornamental pretzels were traditionally given as gifts for New Year's Eve, or presented to children on their first birthday. They were also exhibited during parades and at county fairs under the category of trophy breads, large display pieces with elaborate designs. These pretzels were made of sweetened bread and sometimes filled with nuts and dried fruit. They were also called "potato pretzels" by some Dutch, because the dough used for making them was based on a potato sponge. Our recipe, which was made for Christmas bazaars by Laura Schadler Stofflet (1863-1916) of Fogelsville, Pennsylvania, will produce two large pretzels. You will need an oversized pizza tin to accommodate each pretzel, or two shallow cake tins measuring at least 14 inches (35cm) in diameter. Furthermore, the most traditional decorative design was to ornament the pretzel with three smaller pretzels and three braids representing heads of wheat. Once on display, the pretzels were often additionally decorated with real heads of wheat, barley or spelt, pinecones, and even evergreens; some people added a large bow.

Since the dough used in these pretzels puffs considerably during baking, the trick is to keep the dough on the lean side; otherwise, the pretzel will run together and lose its shape in the oven. Like mastering the Easter Lamb, a few practice runs will be necessary before you get the hang of it, so do not try an elaborate design until you have determined the right combination of baking tin and the quirks of your oven: if there is a hot spot, the pretzel may bake lopsided. Just the same, no matter how it may turn out the first time, Mrs. Stofflet's pretzel recipe will taste just fine. Incidentally, potato water in the ingredient list is water in which potatoes have been boiled. Always save it for your baking needs – you can even freeze it for later use.

Yield: Approximately two 14-inch (35cm) pretzels

½ **ounce (15g) dry active yeast**
1 cup (250ml) lukewarm potato water (98F/37C)
4 tablespoons (60g) unsalted butter
1 cup (170g) light brown sugar
2 large eggs
1 tablespoon (15g) sea salt

1 cup (250ml) milk
1 cup (200g) mashed potatoes
7 cups (875g) bread flour

Glaze for Each Pretzel:
1 egg yolk
1 tablespoon (15ml) cream
1 tablespoon (15g) superfine sugar

Proof the yeast in the lukewarm potato water. In a deep work bowl, cream the butter and brown sugar. Beat the eggs until light and frothy, dissolve the salt in the milk, and add this to the eggs. Add the egg mixture to the butter and sugar, stir well, then stir in the mashed potatoes. Sift in 3 cups (375g) of flour to create a soft sponge. Cover and proof overnight in a warm place until double in bulk.

The next day, stir down and sift in the remaining flour, working batter into soft, pliant dough. Knead for about 10 minutes, then cover and allow the dough to proof until double in bulk. Knock down and divide the dough into two equal portions, each weighing about 2 pounds (1 kg). Trim off excess dough and reserve this for ornamenting the pretzels.

To make a pretzel, take one portion of the dough and roll it out to form a rope about 40 inches (100cm) long. The rope should be thicker in the middle than on the ends. Twist this into a pretzel shape and lay it on your baking tin. Take some of the excess dough and make braids or coils – or roll out some of it as thin as possible with a rolling pin and cut out leaves, petals for flowers, or any fanciful figures you like, and attach them to the pretzel with lightly beaten egg white. Once the design is in place, cover and let the pretzel rise for about 25 to 30 minutes, depending on the warmth of the kitchen.

While the pretzel is rising, preheat the oven to 375F (190C). For each pretzel, beat together the egg yolk, cream and sugar and brush the surface with this. Then bake in the preheated oven for 30 to 35 minutes, or until fully risen and turning golden brown. Cool on a rack. Repeat this with the other portion of dough unless your oven is large enough to accommodate both pretzels at once.

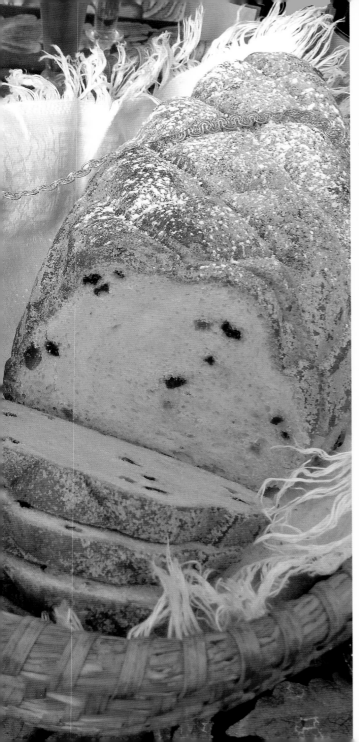

Saffron Bread
Geelbrodt

When the Pennsylvania Dutch first settled in America, the traditional wedding cake among Pennsylvania's Quaker colonials was a type of old English bread flavored with saffron. Throughout Europe, saffron bread in one form or another served as the symbolic luxury food for weddings, funerals, Christmas feasting, New Year's and Easter. The Pennsylvania Dutch – coming as they did from many different parts of German-speaking Europe – also brought their own regional interpretations of this once widespread tradition. For this reason, very early on in the colonial period, saffron bread came to represent a fusion of diverse culinary customs best expressed by the iconic saffron-flavored Schwenkfelder Wedding Cake, which now appears in almost every cookbook claiming to be Pennsylvania Dutch (by virtue of its long-time acceptance in regional cuisine).

For weddings, saffron bread was baked in small round loaves for easier distribution among the guests. In private households, as part of the Christmas celebration for example, the dough was baked as dinner rolls, one per guest. Or, in families that owned fine cake molds, the bread would be baked *Gugelhupf*-style, in an elaborate heirloom mold brought out once a year for this sort of special occasion. I have baked the bread in a rare *Schtriezel* mold, since the braided shape is an old one associated with festive baking. The beauty of saffron bread lies in its seemingly infinite adaptability to meet the needs of many types of special situations. One thing for certain, the bread must be bright yellow, which means no holding back on the saffron!

Finally, a word about the recipe at hand: after viewing hundreds of saffron bread recipes, I settled on Henrietta Pelz's, as adapted from the 1835 edition of her *Schlessisches Kochbuch* (Silesian Cookbook). This is not a Silesian recipe, rather a fairly standard version of saffron bread found in German cookbooks dating from the Renaissance onwards. But it works and works well.

Yield: 16 to 24 servings

1 tablespoon dry active yeast
2 cups (250ml) warm whole milk (98F/37C)
1½ cups (375ml) warm spring water
½ teaspoon ground saffron
8 cups (1 kilo) organic bread flour
4 large eggs
1 cup (250g) sugar
8 tablespoons (125g) unsalted soft butter
1 teaspoon salt
2 teaspoons freshly grated nutmeg, or more to taste
½ cup (75g) Zante currants
½ cup (100g) dried green seedless grapes

Proof the yeast in the warm milk. Once the yeast is foaming, combine it with the warm water in which the saffron has been infused for at least 30 minutes. Place 3 cups (375g) flour in a deep work bowl, then make a valley in the center and add the proofed yeast mixture. Stir to form thin batter. Cover and let rise in a warm place until the batter forms bubbles on the surface. Once covered with bubbles, in a separate bowl, beat the eggs until lemon color and frothy. Add the sugar and beat until creamy, then add the butter, salt and nutmeg. Sift in 4 cups (500g) and work into sticky dough. Cover and let the dough double in bulk. Knock down, and work in the fruit adding only enough extra flour so that the dough does not stick to the fingers.

Form the dough into dinner rolls or fill two earthenware molds, greased and well dusted, with cake crumbs (see note). Whatever your choice, allow the

dough to recover 30 minutes before baking. Bake in an oven preheated to 375F (190C), but the length of time can vary with size: for small rolls, 25 minutes, for bread baked in cake molds, 45 to 50 minutes.

Note: Stale sponge cake or angel cake crumbs are ideal for this purpose. Lacking those options, use unflavored bread crumbs or unsalted cracker crumbs.

Stollen and Strietzel
Schtolle un Schtrietzel

These festive breads are two differently shaped versions of the same thing. The Pennsylvania Dutch prefer to use the term *Schtrietzel*, because the bread is generally baked in the shape of a braid, which is the original medieval meaning of the word (some food historians believe that the braid is symbolic of a head of spelt). Meanwhile, a less common name found in old cookbooks is *Zopp*, which means a pigtail, again in reference to the shape. Unlike stollen, which is mostly associated with Christmas, *Schtrietzel* was originally associated with All Saints (November 1), and since that was also New Year's on the old Celtic calendar, under Christianity it gradually moved over to Christmas and New Year's, and even Easter, thus becoming the iconic festive bread for several different calendrical feast days. On the other hand, *Stollen* is the Saxon German term for the same type of bread baked plain in an oblong, almond-shaped loaf. The stollen shape was mostly sold by bakeries, since they were often owned by immigrant German bakers. Thus, the two forms existed side by side in most parts of the Dutch Country.

Our basic recipe has been supplied by my late Lancaster County friend Ivan Glick (1927-2010) who was well-known for his extraordinary breads and baked goods. Ivan lived in an eighteenth-

Stollen

century log house built by my Weaver ancestors and baked in his mother's old wood-fired stove. He preferred to make *Schtrietzel*, because that is how his Amish grandmother made it. So if you too prefer to make *Schtriezel*, simply divide the batch of dough into three long pieces of equal size and braid them together. Let the braid recover for about 25 minutes and then bake according to the stollen instructions below (or use the Saffron Bread recipe, if you prefer a richer yellow cake). *Schtriezel* is only lightly powdered with confectioner's sugar or not at all; some families scatter poppy seeds over the top before baking. It is considered rich enough without sugar icing. Since the flavor of stollen improves a week or so after it is made, plan ahead to have it on hand in time for Christmas. It also stores for a long time and can be frozen as well.

Yield: Serves about 20 to 25 when sliced

1 tablespoon dry active yeast
2 cups (500ml) warm whole milk (98F/37C)
8 tablespoons (125ml) melted unsalted butter
½ cup (125g) sugar
1 teaspoon salt
8 cups (1 kilo) bread flour
2 teaspoons ground mace
1 cup (150g) Zante currants
1 cup (200g) raisins or sultanas
½ cup (60g) blanched slivered almonds

Proof the yeast in the warm milk. Once it is actively foaming, add the melted butter, sugar and salt. Sift 4 cups (500g) of flour into a deep work bowl and make a valley in the center of the flour. Add the yeast mixture and stir to create thick batter. Cover and let the batter proof in a warm place until covered with bubbles.

Stir down. Sift together the remaining flour and mace, then sift this over the currants, raisins and almonds. Add this to the batter and knead well until it no longer sticks to the fingers, adding more flour if

necessary. Form the loaf into the shape of an almond and lay it on a bread peel dusted with flour. To create the distinctive stollen shape with one side higher than the other, lay a heavy glass or marble rolling pin lengthwise on the left hand half of the loaf – this will create a long dent or "valley." Cover and allow the loaf to recover in a warm place for about 40 to 45 minutes.

When ready to bake, heat the oven to 375F (190C), uncover the loaf and remove the rolling pin. Slide the loaf onto a baking sheet or large pizza tin and bake in the preheated oven for 45 to 50 minutes or until it taps hollow on the bottom. Brush with melted butter as soon as it comes from the oven. When cool, coat liberally with confectioner's sugar flavored with ground cinnamon or cassia.

Sugar Buns or Kissing Buns
Zuckerweck odder Kimmichweck

We have based this recipe on one preserved by Lebanon County furniture maker Peter Ranck (1770-1851). His recipe created a *Fordeeg* (foundation dough) that could then be shaped and baked in any number of ways. Aside from using it for large-scale Dutch Cakes, which were sometimes baked in huge cake pans, another popular form was to make Turkey Buns. These were miniature cakes baked in Turk's Head molds often no more than six inches (15cm) in diameter. Many Pennsylvania Dutch households possessed these little molds, if for no other reason than for using up excess cake batter that might not all fit in a larger cake pan. Bakers often owned sets so that they could make Turkey Buns in batches, and one way to serve them was to soak them in rum: the Pennsylvania Dutch equivalent of Baba au Rhum.

Sugar buns were somewhat different. They were meant to be eaten as finger food (like *Fastnachts*) and were actually placed on the table like dinner rolls, which in the old days meant laying them on the table cloth right beside the dinner plate. Thus, they became the "bread" for the special occasion.

Yield: 10 pairs (20 buns)

½ ounce (15g) dry active yeast
2 cups (500ml) lukewarm whole milk (98F/37C)
5 cups (625g) bread flour
2 teaspoons ground cinnamon
1 tablespoon (5g) freshly grated nutmeg
8 ounces (250g) unsalted butter
1 cup (250g) light brown sugar
½ cup (125ml) rosewater
2 tablespoons (30ml) honey
Coarse sugar (sand sugar or crystal sugar)

Proof the yeast in the milk. While the yeast is proofing, sift together the flour, cinnamon and nutmeg. Set aside. Cream the butter and sugar, then combine this with the proofed yeast and rosewater. Make a valley in the center of the sifted flour and add the butter mixture. Work to form soft, pliant dough. Dust a clean work surface with flour and knead the dough until spongy (about 5 to 8 minutes). Cover and set aside to double in bulk. Knock down and divide the dough into 4-ounce (125g) balls. Set the balls side by side in pairs on ungreased baking sheets. Cover and let the buns rise 20 to 25 minutes.

While the dough is recovering, preheat the oven to 350F (180C). After the buns have risen again, bake them in the preheated oven for approximately 30 minutes or until they tap hollow on the bottom.

While the buns are baking, dissolve the honey in 2 tablespoons (30ml) of hot water. As the buns come out of the oven, immediately brush them with the honey mixture and then scatter sugar over them. Cool on racks.

TWO

CAKES

Kuche

The word *Kuche* in Pennsylvania Dutch can refer to a cake (like a sponge cake), to a pie resembling pizza, and to anything resembling flat bread. What may confuse outsiders is the vast array of cakes the Pennsylvania Dutch have created – especially crumb cakes. And while it may be true that *Hochkuche* (layer cakes) and box cakes have pushed aside some traditional recipes, there are still a great many families who celebrate their cultural identity through desserts like these. Furthermore, just about every farm market in the Dutch Country will feature several stands where local specialties can be found. So we have taken the bakeshop approach in this chapter by selecting the widest possible range of unusual cakes and their stories. Unfortunately, due to space limitations we had to leave quite a number out, like Funny Cake (already well known) and Lydia Bender Cake from Somerset County, which is made with sour cream and covered with fluffy maple sugar icing.

One of the most puzzling pastries both to locals and outsiders is the origin of the cake known as apeas – we have included several examples in this chapter. There are two distinct types: one is a cookie, either a drop cookie or a roll-out cookie; the other is a crumb cake generally eaten with coffee. The seed cookies were flavored with anise and sold in the streets by vendors, but since many "English" (non-Dutch) did not like anise, a separate batch was always prepared with caraway, which the non-Dutch found acceptable. The caraway cookie, stamped with the letters A.P., was also known as Philadelphia Seed Cake, because it was once popular as a street food in the city's open-air markets. However, the cake called apeas has a more unusual past.

Its name evolved from *Anis Plätschen* sometime in the early nineteenth century. In the cookie chapter, I have included an 1858 recipe for the true original anise drop cookie that was made and sold by many Pennsylvania Dutch bakers. If you take a cupful of that cookie batter and bake it in a 7-inch (18cm) tin – the traditional apeas cake size – you will get the anise-flavored crumb cake from which all the variant cakes now descend. Conversely, you can make drop cookies from any of the apeas cake recipes in this book.

The original creative transition from anise to other flavorings was simple and shaped by local Pennsylvania Dutch taste preferences: saffron apeas cakes from Lebanon County, vanilla apeas from Lehigh and Northampton, and buckwheat apeas from Cumberland and Perry County. The variations seem endless and there is nothing quite like them in the Old World – further proof (if such is needed) that Pennsylvania Dutch cookery is thoroughly American.

In addition to a collection of rare apeas recipes, I have also included a classic cake recipe from the manuscript household book of Mary Hamilton Winebrenner (1808-1888), the second wife of Reverend John Winebrenner, founder of the Church of God in Harrisburg, Pennsylvania. Mrs. Winebrenner's Leopard Cake is as spotted and as unusual as its name implies. Like Bishop's Bread (our second recipe in this chapter), both are the sort of tour-de-force desserts that were symbols of the parlor culture of the old Pennsylvania Dutch social elites.

Lastly, go to the special effort of locating caster sugar, also known as bar sugar or superfine sugar. This type of quick-dissolving sugar was used in many old recipes under the name of "rolled sugar" or "powdered sugar." It was employed in cake baking because it yielded a finer, more delicate texture than common granulated sugar, and you should notice the difference when you use it.

Bigler Cake
Bigler Kuche

This deliciously moist and crumbly cake is historically important for several reasons. First, the cake was named in honor of William Bigler (1814-1880), a Pennsylvania Dutch governor of Pennsylvania who served from 1852 to 1855 – his brother was elected the first governor of California at the very same time. Bigler then became a U.S. Senator from 1856 to 1861 and played an important role in national politics leading up to the Civil War. The original recipe for the cake was included in the 1869 *Book of Recipes* published at Gettysburg, the first Pennsylvania Dutch cookbook devoted exclusively to cakes and pastries.

Bigler Cake represents a creative turning point, a break with older, more traditional types of spice cakes. While its novelty in the 1850s may have recommended it to the followers of changing fashion, it remains a classic if its kind. There are two traditional ways of baking it: plain (in pie tins) or fancy (in a cake mold).

Recommended utensils: two 8-inch (20cm) pie pans or a Bundt mold.

Yield: Serves 8 to 10

3 cups (375g) cake flour
1 cup (250g) sugar
1 tablespoon baking powder
1 teaspoon salt
Grated zest of 2 lemons
6 tablespoons (90g) unsalted butter
2 eggs
1½ cups (375ml) buttermilk
Coarse sugar or lemon crumbs as topping

Grease the pie pans or cake mold and set aside. Preheat the oven to 375F (190C). Sift together the flour, sugar, baking powder and salt, then add the lemon zest. Make a valley in the center of the dry ingredients. Melt the butter and pour it into the valley. Beat the eggs until lemon colored and frothy, then combine with the buttermilk. Add this to the melted butter and stir the ingredients to form stiff, sticky batter. Pour this into the prepared pie pans or a cake mold that has been greased and dusted with bread or cake crumbs. If using pie pans, sprinkle crumbs over the tops; if using a mold, ice the cake once it is cool. Bake in the preheated oven for 30 to 35 minutes or until fully puffed and set in the middle. If baking in a Bundt mold, bake for 35-40 minutes. Serve at room temperature.

Bishop's Bread

Bishop's Bread
Bischoffs Brod

The name of this cake alludes to a time prior to the Civil War, when Bishop's Bread was originally made with yeast and thus more like the sweetened breads in the first chapter of this book. It was also a special occasion cake, as the name might imply. In this case, the bishop was Amish, since the recipe comes from the Amish community around Belleville in the Big Valley of Mifflin County. It was one of those cakes made only for entertaining special guests, like the bishop and his wife, or for Amish weddings, or for Twelfth Night, which the Amish call Old Christmas.

Recommended utensils: two 10-inch (25cm) cake tins with tall sides, or one earthenware *Schales* pan, as called for in the original recipe.

Yield: 12 to 16

2½ cups (315g) cake flour
1 cups (185g) brown sugar
1 teaspoon salt
8 tablespoons (125g) unsalted butter
¼ cup (35g) chopped almonds
½ cup (100g) chopped apricots
1 tablespoon baking powder
1 teaspoon ground cinnamon
Grated zest and juice of 1 orange
2 large eggs
½ teaspoon baking soda
1 cup (250ml) buttermilk

Topping:
½ cup (35g) sliced almonds

Preheat the oven to 400F (200C). Sift together the flour, sugar and salt. Rub in the butter to create uniform crumbs. Remove ¾ cup (125g) of the crumbs, then combine the remaining crumbs with the chopped almonds and apricots. Add the baking powder, cinnamon and orange zest. Then beat the eggs until lemon colored and frothy and add the orange juice. Dissolve the soda in the buttermilk and add this to the eggs. Pour the liquid into a valley in the middle of the crumbs and beat until smooth. Pour the batter into two greased cake tins. Combine the reserved crumbs with the sliced almonds and scatter over the top. Bake in the preheated oven for 25 minutes or until fully risen and set in the center.

Watch Point: If your oven bakes hot, you may have trouble with scorching. To avoid this, try baking the cakes at 325F (165C) for 50 minutes to an hour.

Breitinger's Apple Cake with Cheese
Breitingers Ebbel-un-Kees Kuche

Is it a cake or a pudding? It's a little bit of both. This famous Pennsylvania Dutch dessert from Breitinger's Dining Saloons in Harrisburg is the epitome of old-fashioned comfort food. You can even add a little more grated Parmesan cheese to the breadcrumbs, or for a more complex flavor, combine a few sliced figs with the apples. The original recipe was preserved by Mary Hessenberger (1850-1944), whose husband, Charles, was for many years the proprietor of Breitinger's.

Suggested Utensil: a 10-inch (25cm) diameter flat-bottomed spring-form sponge cake tin with a center tube. The sides should be at least 4 inches (10cm) deep, because the batter puffs considerably during baking.

Yield: Serves 6 to 8

8 eggs, yolks and whites separated
8 tablespoons (126g) superfine sugar
  (also called caster sugar)
1½ tablespoon baking powder
1½ cups (185g) breadcrumbs
¾ cup (90g) grated Parmesan cheese
½ cup (125ml) fresh lemon juice
2 to 3 apples, cored and sliced paper thin
  (leave the skins on)
2 teaspoon freshly ground mace
2 cups (200g) shredded sharp cheese
  (Cheddar type)

Preheat the oven to 350F (180C). Grease a cake pan and dust it liberally with breadcrumbs. Set aside.

Cream the egg yolks and sugar. Combine the baking powder, salt, breadcrumbs and Parmesan cheese, then add this to the eggs and sugar and mix thoroughly. Add the lemon juice. Beat the egg whites until stiff and forming peaks, and fold them into the batter.

Pour about 1/3 of the batter on the bottom of the prepared cake pan, then make a layer of sliced apples. Sprinkle some of the shredded cheese and mace over this. Make another layer of batter, then another layer of apples, sprinkled with the cheese and mace. Continue in this fashion until all the ingredients are used: the top layer should consist of a thick layer of batter with some of the remaining shredded cheese scattered over it.

Bake in the preheated oven for 40 to 45 minutes or until the cake tests dry with a skewer or broom straw. Serve at room temperature.

Coffee Shoofly Cake
Kaffee Schuflei Kuche

Our recipe for this delicious cake has come down to us from Carolina Levan Reber, in her day one of the best-known country cooks in the Reading area. However, Mrs. Reber's cake is not the same as the pie of similar name. Her cake is the closest heirloom recipe we have to the original Centennial Cake, introduced in 1876, and which later morphed into the now-iconic molasses pie. Like Buttermilk Crumb Pie (page 118), Coffee Shoofly Cake was baked in a square pan, the suggested dimension being 9 by 9 inches (23 by 23cm).

The pie and Mrs. Reber's cake take their name from a once-famous boxing mule called Shoofly, whose name incidentally created a pun in Pennsylvania Dutch, since *Schufli* is also a little crumb – the main ingredient in both the pie and cake. During the 1870s and 1880s, Shoofly the mule was part of a traveling circus act in the Dutch Country, and he is depicted in the late 1870s Lancaster trade card on page 185.

Yield: Serves 8 to 10

Crumb Topping:
½ cup (65g) all-purpose flour
¼ cup (65g) coarse organic sugar
2 tablespoons (30g) unsalted butter

Cake Part:
2½ cups (315g) all-purpose flour
1 cup (170g) light brown sugar
2 teaspoons baking powder
1 teaspoon ground cinnamon
1 teaspoon grated nutmeg
¼ teaspoon ground cloves
8 tablespoons (125g) unsalted butter
1 egg, separated

1 cup (250ml) barrel molasses
1 teaspoon baking soda
1 cup (250ml) hot black coffee
  (the stronger the better)
1 cake bitter chocolate

Preheat the oven to 350F (175C) and prepare the crumb topping first. Rub together the flour, sugar and butter to create fine crumbs and set aside.

In a large work bowl, prepare the cake batter by sifting together the flour, brown sugar, baking powder, cinnamon, nutmeg and cloves. Work in the butter to form loose crumbs.

In another work bowl, beat the egg yolk until lemon colored and frothy, then whisk in the molasses. Dissolve the baking soda in the hot coffee, then combine this with the molasses. Add this to the crumb mixture and stir gently to create a thick batter. Beat the egg white until it forms peaks, then fold it into the batter. Grease your cake pan and add the batter, spreading it evenly over the bottom. Scatter the reserved crumb topping over the batter and bake in the preheated oven for 45 to 50 minutes until fully risen and set in the center. Cool on a rack and serve at room temperature, liberally garnished with tiny shreds of bitter chocolate. Use an apple peeler to create the shreds.

Coffee Spice Cake
Kaffee Gewaertz Kuche

I thought the preceding coffee cake recipe would satisfy our cravings, but things get even better with this delicious cake from the Big Valley in Mifflin County, Pennsylvania. It came to us from the late Lydia M. Yoder (1918-2000), a member of the Allensville Mennonite community in that area.

Her recipe was easy to locate because it is the same popular cake that was served during the 1960s under the name Amish Spice Cake at the Water Gate Inn in Washington, D.C. Mocha icing with bits of caramelized sugar scattered over the top is a perfect match with strong coffee, but Big Valley cooks prefer powdered sugar.

Yield: Serves 8 to 10

½ cup (125g) unsalted butter
1 cup (175g) light brown sugar
3 eggs, yolks and whites separated
½ cup (125ml) strong black coffee, room
  temperature
1½ cups (190g) cake flour
2 teaspoons baking powder
1 teaspoon ground cinnamon
1 teaspoon freshly grated nutmeg
½ teaspoon ground cloves
Confectioners (10-X) sugar

Preheat the oven to 350F (180C). Grease a 10-inch (23cm) cake tin and dust it with breadcrumbs or cake crumbs. Set aside.

Cream the butter and sugar, beating vigorously until all the sugar is dissolved. Beat the egg yolks until lemon colored and frothy, then add the coffee. Combine this with the creamed butter and sugar, again beating vigorously so that the ingredients do not separate.

Sift together the flour, baking powder, cinnamon, nutmeg and cloves. Make a valley in the center of the dry ingredients and add the liquid ingredients. Stir to create a thick, creamy batter. Whisk the egg whites until they form stiff peaks, then fold them into the batter. Pour this into the prepared cake tin and bake in the preheated oven for 25 to 30 minutes or until set in the center. Remove from the oven, dust with confectioners sugar and cool on a rack.

Crumb Cake
Grimmelkuche

I would be remiss if I did not include at least one classic crumb cake in this collection. After testing many recipes from different parts of the Dutch Country, this one stood out as easy-to-make and flexible in terms of presentation. I leave flavoring to your imagination, although vanilla is called for in the original.

Our recipe traces to the late Helen Fenstermacher Breidigam of Lyons, Pennsylvania, wife of Delight R. Breidigam, Sr., co-founder of the East Penn Manufacturing Company, in Lyons. Her recipe has been widely circulated among church groups in southern Berks County and was a featured cake at fundraisers for Christ Lutheran Church in Dryville, where she was a member. Mrs. Breidigam baked her cakes in three 7-inch (18cm) tins, which was the traditional way to prepare them as breakfast cakes – much in the same manner as apeas.

Yield: Serves 8 to 10

3 cups (375g) all-purpose flour
1¾ cups (435g) sugar
2 teaspoons baking powder
1 teaspoon salt
12 tablespoons (180g) unsalted butter
2 eggs
1¼ cups (315ml) clabbered raw milk or buttermilk
2 teaspoons vanilla

Sift together the flour, sugar, salt and baking powder. Rub the butter into this to form fine crumbs. Set aside 1/3 cup (35g) of the crumbs. Beat the eggs until lemon colored then combine with the milk and vanilla. Add this to the crumb mixture to create batter. Grease and dust with breadcrumbs three 7-inch (18cm) pie tins. Fill them one-half full and top with the reserved crumbs. Bake at 400F for 20 to 25 minutes or until fully risen and set in the middle.

Dutch Apple Cake

Dutch Apple Cake
Deitscher Ebbelkuche

This elegant yet simple cake came to us from McVey-town in Mifflin County, Pennsylvania, where it was long associated with its originator, Phoebe Hanawalt (1884-1958), wife of a well known Church of the Brethren minister. The cake is best when baked in a 10 to 11-inch (25 to 28cm) *Schales* pan or cake tin of similar proportions with 1-inch (2.5cm) sides.

Yield: 8 to 10

2 cups (250g) cake flour
1 teaspoon salt
2 teaspoons baking powder
1½ tablespoons (25g) sugar
4 tablespoons (60g) unsalted butter
½ cup (50g) chopped hickory nuts
Grated zest of 1 lemon
2 eggs
1 cup (250ml) whole milk
3 to 4 apples, pared, cored and quartered (number of apples depends on their size)
Cold butter
1 tablespoon coarse sugar
½ teaspoon ground cinnamon

Preheat the oven to 350F (180C). Sift together the dry ingredients, then work the butter to a crumb in a food processor or with a pastry cutter. Set aside in a deep work bowl and add the nuts and lemon zest. Beat the eggs until light and frothy, then combine with the milk. Make a valley in the center of the dry ingredients and add the egg-milk mixture. Work this into a stiff batter and pour it into a greased 10 to 11-inch (25 to 28cm) *Schales* pan or cake tin with 1-inch (2.5cm) sides. Press the quartered apples cut-side down into the batter, arranging them in a circular pattern. Slash each apple with 8 or 10 deep vertical cuts. Dot each piece of apple with a small square of butter, combine the sugar and cinnamon and scatter this evenly over the apples and cake. Bake in the preheated oven 30-35 minutes. Serve hot from the oven or at room temperature.

Note: Any sort of fresh fruit can be used as topping with this batter.

Dutch Butter Cake
Budderkuche odder Dickemillich Kuche

Dutch Butter Cake or "German" Butter Cake, as it is sometimes called, are the common commercial names for a popular cake peculiar to the Dutch Country and still produced by many local bakeries. Known as *Dickemillich Kuche* (Clabber Cake) in Pennsylfaanisch, it was often sweetened with honey instead of sugar. Some recipes call for a gooey topping of melted sugar and butter. That is the way it was served during the 1920s at Chef's, a chicken-and-waffles restaurant at Annville, Pennsylvania. I have decided to keep it simple, like the farmhouse recipes of 100 years ago.

Yield: 8 to 10 Servings

½ ounce (15g) dry active yeast
½ cup (125ml) lukewarm milk
1 teaspoon sugar
8 tablespoons (125g) unsalted butter, room temperature
½ cup (125g) sugar
1 teaspoon salt
1 cup (250ml) sour cream or yoghurt
2 large eggs
2 cups (250g) bread flour
3 tablespoons (45g) cold, unsalted butter chopped into tiny bits
2 tablespoons (30g) coarse granulated sugar
1 teaspoon powdered cinnamon or cassia

Proof the yeast in the milk slightly sweetened with 1 teaspoon sugar. Cream the butter, remaining sugar and salt, then add the sour cream. Beat the eggs until lemon colored and frothy, then whisk vigorously into the batter. Add the proofed yeast, then sift in the flour to form a soft, sticky sponge. Cover and set aside in a warm place until double in bulk.

Preheat the oven to 375F (190C), then stir down the sponge. Grease a 10 by 2 by 10 (23 by 5 by 23 cm) cake pan (or two 8-inch/20cm square pans) and dust liberally with breadcrumbs. Add the proofed sponge, spreading it evenly in the pan. Cover with a warm damp cloth and allow the sponge to recover in a warm place until the cake has risen almost to the top edge of the pan. Remove the cloth and dot the top with the chopped butter. Combine the cinnamon or cassia and sugar and then scatter this over the cake. Bake for 30 to 35 minutes or until the cake tests done in the center. Cool before cutting.

Watch Point: If the cake appears to be darkening too much on the top, cover it with a sheet of tin foil to prevent scorching. Do not remove the cake from the oven prematurely, or it will fall.

Dutch Butter Cake

Filled Crumb Cake
G'fillte Schtreiselkuche

While it might be argued that in this chapter we have explored crumb cakes to the very last crumb, there always seems to be one more recipe with an interesting twist and new take on the concept. Our recipe here comes from Lena H. Lebo (1879-1971), who lived in western Chester County, right on the border of the Dutch Country. She descended from an old Huguenot family that came to Pennsylvania from Alsace. This is a Lebo family recipe, and what makes it special is that different crumbs go inside as well as on top; thus, it is multi-textured. There is a whole branch of crumb cake cookery in which the cakes are filled in some manner, be it a thin layer of apple butter, quince honey or peach preserves – or in this case, with a rich nut-crumb mixture. Some Dutch like gooey centers, others do not. Hopefully, this recipe will strike an acceptable middle ground.

Yield: Serves 8 to 10

Filling:
½ **cup (90g) brown sugar**
1 **tablespoon ground cinnamon**
2 **tablespoons (15g) cake flour**
2 **tablespoons (15ml) melted unsalted butter**
½ **cup (60g) chopped hickory nuts or hazelnuts**

Combine these ingredients in a work bowl, stirring them together with a horn or wooden fork, then set aside. Preheat the oven to 375 F (190C).

Cake Part:
1½ **cups (185g) cake flour**
1 **tablespoon baking powder**
¼ **teaspoon salt**
¾ **cup (185g) sugar**
4 **tablespoons (60g) unsalted butter or lard**
1 **egg**
½ **cup (125ml) whole milk**

While the oven is heating, sift together the flour, baking powder, salt and sugar, then rub in the butter or lard to create crumbs. Beat the egg until light and frothy, and combine with the milk. Make a valley in the center of the crumb mixture and add the liquid ingredients to form thick, sticky batter. Spread half the batter in bottom of a well-greased cake tin, then cover this with half of the reserved crumb mixture. Cover with the remaining cake batter and sprinkle the rest of the crumbs on top. Bake in the preheated oven for 35 to 40 minutes or until the cake tests done in the center.

Observation: For best visual appearance, bake in deep 6 or 7-inch (15 or 18cm) cake tins or in a small square one.

Gerhart's Reunion Cake

Gerharts Rieyunien Kuche

Family reunions are major events in the Dutch Country, and quite often, a focal point for special foods made for the occasion. One of the oldest continuous family reunions celebrates the coming of Johann Gerhart to Pennsylvania in 1739. Sometime in the early 1900s, a cake was created for the annual picnic held in his honor.

Our recipe traces to Susan Weinhold Gerhart (1857-1934) of Wernersville, Pennsylvania, who wrote down the recipe in 1927. It would appear, however, that it is based on or derived from an 1850s cornstarch cake made famous throughout the Dutch Country by Annie Wampole of Norristown, Pennsylvania. Mrs. Wampole's cake took blue ribbons at country fairs and her award-winning recipe was widely published in local newspapers. Like Mrs. Wampole's cake, the Gerhart cake is light, somewhat like sponge cake. It was not iced, because it was served with ice cream and strawberries, or whatever fruit was in season. The most common choice of flavoring was lemon or bitter almond.

Yield: Serves 8 to 10

8 tablespoons (125g) unsalted butter
1 cup (250g) caster sugar (also called bar sugar)
flavoring of your choice (about 1 teaspoon)
½ cup (125ml) butter milk
1¼ cups (155g) double-sifted cake flour
¾ cup (90g) potato starch
1 tablespoon baking powder
¼ teaspoon salt
3 egg whites

Preheat the oven to 375F (190C). Cream the butter and sugar until light and fluffy. Add the flavoring of your choice and the buttermilk. In a separate work bowl, sift together the cake flour, potato starch, baking powder and salt. Sift and fold this into the wet ingredients to create smooth batter. Beat the egg whites until they form stiff peaks, then fold them into the batter.

Pour the batter into a greased 10-inch (26cm) cake pan with a center tube or a loaf pan and bake in the preheated oven for 40 minutes or until it tests done. Cool on a rack before removing from the pan.

Watch Point: If you do not double-sift the cake flour before measuring it, this cake is likely to bake dry.

Honey Loaf Cake with Walnuts
Hunnichkuche mit Walnisse

Years ago, this old-fashioned loaf cake baked in bread or scrapple pans was prepared a week or two before the holiday season, because it needed to age for improved flavor. Since there is no shortening in the dough, this is also relatively low-fat, as cakes go. After aging, the cake becomes denser and more flavorful; it can even be stored in cheesecloth dipped in rum or brandy. However, the most common treatment was to slice it as thin as possible and then cut each slice into wedges for eating with coffee, nuts or dessert wine. It also makes an excellent tea cake when eaten with butter or a mixture of honey and butter.

Yield: 10 to 15 servings (when sliced very thin)

1 cup (250ml) honey
2½ cups (325g) all-purpose flour
1½ tablespoons baking powder
1 teaspoon ground cinnamon
1 teaspoon ground cardamom
½ teaspoon salt
3 large eggs
¾ cup (125g) light brown sugar
1 cup (125g) chopped walnuts

Grease two small bread pans and dust with cake crumbs or fine breadcrumbs. Set aside. Preheat the oven to 375F (190C).

Warm the honey in a pan of lukewarm water so that it liquefies. Sift together the flour, baking powder and spices. In a separate bowl, beat the eggs until lemon colored and frothy, then beat in the sugar until the mixture is creamy and the sugar fully dissolved. Sift in the flour mixture to form a thick batter, then add the honey. Lastly, fold in the chopped nuts. Pour the batter into the prepared loaf pans and bake in the preheated oven for 45 to 50 minutes or until fully risen and set in the middle. When done, remove from

the pans and cool on a rack. Then, wrap the cakes in baking parchment and store in a tight container to ripen at least 1 week before serving.

Note: The most ideal baking pans for this cake is the type of loaf pan with a sliding lid. This will insure that the cake is perfectly rectangular. However the batter can also be baked in a small Turk's Head mold with a center tube, or in a spring form cake tin with center tube.

Hyndman Corn Cake
Heindman Welschkarn Kuche

This delightful old-time Bedford County recipe from one of the sparsely settled Dutch valleys has been modernized for baking in a 9-inch (23cm) spring form cake tin. The original was baked in a spider or in a cast iron skillet on the hearth floor ("down hearth") – rather than on a raised hearth, the traditional Dutch way. Our cornmeal of choice is triple-sifted flour from Iroquois "Tooth Corn" (Gourdseed Corn), tracing to the Cornplanter Senecas of

Allegheny County, but any good organic white cornmeal will suffice. The maple sugar in this recipe comes from Somerset County and can be ordered from the producer on page 174.

Yield: Serves 8 to 10

1¾ cups (215g) all-purpose flour
¾ cup (125g) fine white cornmeal
4 tablespoons (65g) maple sugar
1 teaspoon salt
1 tablespoon (5g) baking powder
2 eggs
1¼ cup (315ml) buttermilk
3 tablespoons (45ml) melted unsalted butter or lard
Maple sugar
Caraway seeds

Preheat the oven to 400F (200C). Sift together the flour, cornmeal, sugar, salt and baking powder. Beat the eggs until frothy and lemon colored and then add the buttermilk and melted butter. Combine the dry and wet ingredients to form soft sticky dough. Grease a spring form cake pan and dust it liberally with fine cracker crumbs or semolina. Fill with the dough and spread it out with the back of a spoon dipped in water. Scatter maple sugar and caraway seeds over the top and bake in the preheated oven for 30 minutes or until fully set in the center. Remove from the cake tin and cool on a rack. Best eaten the day it is made.

Leopard Cake
Lepperkuche

This unusual recipe was discovered in the extensive manuscript cookbook begun in 1837 by Mary Winebrenner (1808-1888), wife of Harrisburg minister John Winebrenner (1797-1860), founder of the Church of God. We have dipped into her collection because Mary Winebrenner was a notable social figure in the state capital, and judging from the multitudes of cake recipes that captured her attention, she must have been quite an entertainer. As for Leopard Cake, it is essentially two separate types of cake (sponge cake and fruit cake) combined into one, thus creating the spotted appearance. You can bake it either in a loaf pan or in a 10-inch (25cm) spring form cake tin with a center tube. Either way, be certain to line your baking pan with baking parchment so the cake is easier to remove. Furthermore, for best results, all ingredients should be at room temperature.

Yield: Serves 10 to 12

To Make the White Part:
1 cup (250g) caster sugar (also called bar sugar)
1 cup (250g) unsalted butter
8 egg whites (reserve the yolks for the brown part)
1 teaspoon lemon flavoring or to taste
2 cups (250g) cake flour
1 teaspoon baking powder

Preheat the oven to 325F (165C). Cream the butter and sugar, then beat the egg whites until stiff and forming peaks. Fold the whites into the butter mixture and add the flavoring. Sift together the flour and baking powder, then sift and fold this into the batter. Set aside and proceed with the brown part.

To Make the Brown Part:
1½ cups (250g) dark brown sugar
1 cup (250g) unsalted butter
8 egg yolks (reserved from the whites above)
2 cups (250g) cake flour
1 teaspoon ground cinnamon
½ teaspoon ground cloves
1 teaspoon baking powder
8 ounces (250g) Zante currants

In a separate work bowl, cream the brown sugar and butter until light and fluffy. Beat the yolks until thick and creamy, then fold them into the butter mixture. Sift together the flour, cinnamon, cloves and baking powder, then sift and fold this into the batter. Dust the currants with a little flour, then fold them into the batter.

Grease and line your baking tin with baking parchment. Pour half of the white batter on the bottom. Make scoops of the brown batter with a small dipper; drop the scoops in an irregular patter onto the white batter, using only half of the brown batter. Cover this with the remaining white batter, then drop scoopfuls of the remaining brown batter on top. This should fill your baking tin 2/3 full; more than that and it may overflow. Bake in the preheated oven for 55 to 60 minutes or until the cake tests done in the center. Cool on a rack before removing from the pan. The cake is ornamental enough with its spotted appearance, but you may drizzle Madeira or caramel flavored icing over it for added visual effect and flavor.

Observation: While we have followed Mrs. Winebrenner's recipe as faithfully as possible, we suggest that there be a change: Instead of pouring half of the white batter on the bottom, add the batters in alternating ¼-cup scoops. This will create a more patchy visual effect, and the two batters are not likely to separate during baking.

Maple Sugar Apeas
Eepieskuche fun Ahornzucker

Many years ago, when I was working on *Pennsylvania Dutch Country Cooking*, I put out word that I was interested in locating recipes from the southern half or "Dutch End" of Somerset County. A few months later, I received a packet of recipes from Lola Hollanda Showalter (1934-1997), a member of the Church of the Brethren in a little place called Springs, Pennsylvania. Just across the border in Maryland, Lola had relatives who heard about my quest for recipes. They got in touch with her, and then out of the blue, she mailed me a raft of wonderful cake recipes, including this one for maple sugar apeas. We have revised the recipe to conform to our easy-to-make formula. Otherwise, it retains the character of Lola's original: the delightful maple flavor is reminiscent of caramel ice cream.

Yield: Three 7-inch (18cm) cakes

3 cups (375g) pastry flour
1 cup (250g) finely granulated maple sugar
2 tablespoons baking powder
½ teaspoon salt
¾ cup (75g) finely chopped toasted hickory nuts
    (reserve ¼ cup/25g for topping)
6 tablespoons (90g) unsalted butter or
3 tablespoons (45g) unsalted butter, plus
    3 tablespoons (45g) of maple cream
2 eggs
1½ cups (375ml) sour cream

Topping:
2 tablespoons maple sugar
¼ cup (25g) reserved toasted hickory nuts
    (see above)

Grease the pie dishes and set aside. Preheat the oven to 375F (190C). Sift together flour, sugar, baking powder and salt. Add ½ cup (50g) of the hickory nuts. Make a valley in the center of the dry ingredients. Melt the butter and pour it into the valley. Beat the eggs until lemon colored, then combine with the sour cream. Pour this into the valley and, using a fork, work the mixture into sticky dough. Divide into 3 equal parts and place them on the prepared pie pans. Spread smooth and even the edges with the back of a wet spoon. Combine the 2 tablespoons of maple sugar and remaining hickory nuts for the topping and scatter this evenly over the cakes. Bake in the preheated oven for 20 minutes or until fully puffed and set in the middle. Cool on racks.

Osterburg Easter Cake
Oschterbarrick Oschterkuche

Unless you live there, most people do not realize that Osterburg is a Pennsylvania Dutch settlement in Bedford County. Hans Oster settled it in 1771; his grandson William laid out the village in 1876. By happy coincidence, this Easter cake originated in the small German town of Osterburg in Saxony-Anhalt.

While it has no direct connection to the Pennsylvania Oster family that we know of, the original Osterburg Easter Cake claims many lineal descendants in Pennsylvania, including Moravian Sugar Cake. Moravian Sugar Cake, which appears in many of our regional cookbooks, evolved out of the Osterburg prototype.

We decided to publish this delicious cake recipe because it appears in the 1778 cookbook of sugar heiress Catherine Schaeffer Muhlenberg (1750-1835), the wife of Frederick Augustus Muhlenberg, first Speaker of the House of Representatives. Muhlenberg family recipes are now experiencing a lively revival of interest, because the historic Muhlenberg farmhouse in Trappe, Pennsylvania, has undergone restoration with the intention of showcasing the daily life and culinary arts for which Mrs. Muhlenberg was once so famous. And lastly, if you want to decorate this the traditional way with red eggs, press plain hard-cooked eggs with shells intact into the dough before it goes into the oven. After the cake is baked, remove the eggs and replace them with hard-cooked eggs dyed red.

Yield: Serves 10 to 16

½ **ounce (15g) dry active yeast**
½ **cup (125ml) lukewarm potato water**
4 **tablespoons (60g) unsalted butter**
1 **cup (250g) superfine sugar**
2 **large eggs**
2 **teaspoons sea salt**
1 **cup (250ml) sour cream**
½ **cup (100g) mashed potatoes**
5 **cups (625g) bread flour**
⅓ **cup (80ml) rosewater**
½ **cup (75g) Zante currants**
2 **tablespoons grated nutmeg**

Glaze for Crust:
1 **strained egg yolk**
1 **tablespoon (15ml) cream**

Topping:
2 **ounces (65g) unsalted butter**
¼ **cup (60g) coarse sugar**
1 **tablespoon ground cinnamon or ground cardamom**

Proof the yeast in the lukewarm potato water. In a deep work bowl, cream the butter and the sugar. Beat the eggs until light and frothy, dissolve the salt in the sour cream and add this to the eggs. Add the egg mixture to the butter and sugar, stir well, then stir in the mashed potatoes. Sift in 3 cups (375g) of flour to create a soft sponge. Cover and proof overnight in a warm place until double in bulk.

The next day, stir down and add the rosewater and currants. Sift together the remaining flour and nutmeg, then add this to the proofed batter, working it into soft, pliant dough. Knead for about 10 minutes, then cover and allow the dough to proof until double in bulk. Knock down and roll out into a large disc, approximately 1-inch (2.5cm) thick. Lay the dough in a greased baking tin measuring 14 to 15 inches (35 to 38cm) in diameter. Press the edges up to form a narrow border crust. Cover and let the dough recover for 25 to 30 minutes.

While the dough is recovering, preheat the oven to 350F (180C). Beat together the egg yolk and cream and brush the crust border with this. Chop the butter into small bits and scatter these over the top of the cake. Then, mix the sugar and cinnamon and dust the cake with this. Bake in the preheated oven for 30 to 35 minutes or until fully risen and turning golden brown. Cool on a rack. This cake can be frozen for later use.

Railroad Cake
Reggelweg Kuche

This wonderful old-fashioned cake with a very dense, buttery crumb was first published in *The Gettysburg Centennial Cookbook* in 1876. It went from there to become one of the most popular regional cakes during the rest of the century, doubtless because it was an easy sell at picnics and church bazaars. It took its name from the fact that in the days before parlor cars, the cake was sold by hucksters (mostly women) at train stations along the Pennsylvania Railroad. The original idea was to eat it as finger food with a swab of jam or jelly.

Yield: Serves 8 to 10

2 cups (250g) cake flour
1 teaspoon cream of tartar
1 teaspoon baking soda
¼ teaspoon salt
¾ cup (180g) unsalted butter
1 cup (250g) sugar
3 eggs
6 tablespoons (90ml) buttermilk
Finely grated zest of 1 lemon

Preheat the oven to 350F (180C). Sift together the flour, cream of tartar, baking soda and salt and set aside. In separate work bowl, cream the butter and sugar until light and fluffy. Beat the eggs until lemon colored, add the buttermilk and beat in the butter and sugar mixture. Gradually sift in the mixed dry ingredients, working the batter gently with a paddle until smooth. Add the lemon zest.

Grease a 10½-inch (26cm) cake pan with 1-inch (2.5cm) high sides. Dust it liberally with fine breadcrumbs or finely ground cake crumbs. Add the batter and spread it evenly in the pan. Bake in the preheated oven for 25-30 minutes or until turning golden on top and set in the center. Serve at room temperature plain or with icing.

This has led to a waggish expression in Pennsylvania Dutch: *wo die Buwe rauh sin, un die Meedel faddich* – which translates to: Rough and Ready: where the boys are rough and the girls are ready. Betty Klinger Erdman (1927-1996) laughed with a little sparkle in her eye when she repeated that saying and added in Dutch: *awwer unsri Meedel besser backe!* (but our girls are better at baking). Well, the girls do bake in Rough and Ready, and the bake sales at the village's nearby churches stand in lasting testimony to that. One of the local favorites is Rough-and-Ready Cake, which is flavored and colored brazen flamingo pink with teaberry candies. Mrs. Erdman kindly provided the recipe when I interviewed her in 1992.

Rough-and-Ready Cake
Rauh-un-Faddich Kuche

Rough and Ready is a Pennsylvania Dutch village in Schuylkill County. It is named after a gold rush town in California, because a gold mine was discovered near the village about the same time, and everyone thought a payload was in the making. Those riches never materialized, yet the name stuck, because it originally referred to the nickname of President Zachary Taylor, "Old Rough and Ready." In any case, the village traces back to the 1850s and has added considerable local color to the area.

Yield: Serves 8 to 10

8 ounces (250g) teaberries (small candy berries) or 4 ounces (125g) teaberries, plus a few drops of wintergreen flavoring
1½ cups (375ml) lukewarm milk (98F/37C)
1 cup (250g) sugar
½ cup (125g) shortening (unsalted butter)
3 cups (375g) cake flour
1 tablespoon baking powder
4 egg whites

Preheat the oven to 350F (180C). Grease a spring-form cake pan with a center tube and dust it with flour or fine cake crumbs. Set aside.

Dissolve the teaberry candies in the milk, then allow the milk to cool to room temperature. Cream the sugar and shortening until light and fluffy. Add the teaberry milk and whisk smooth. Sift together the flour and the baking powder, then sift this into the liquid ingredients. Beat the egg whites until stiff and forming peaks, and fold them into the batter. Pour the batter into the prepared cake pan and bake in the preheated oven for approximately 45 to 50 minutes or until the cake is done in the center. Remove and cool on a rack, then turn out of the pan to cool for icing.

Picnic Icing:

Once the cake has cooled, prepare Picnic Icing, which is better adapted to the rigors of humid summer weather.

Yield: Enough for one cake

5 tablespoons (75ml) milk
4 ounces (125g) teaberries or more to taste
Red food coloring (optional)
1 large egg
2 cups (500g) sugar
2 teaspoons soft unsalted butter
Teaberries for garnish

Put the milk in a small work bowl and dissolve the teaberries in it. Add red food coloring if you want a darker pink color for the icing. Once the teaberries are dissolved, beat the egg until lemon colored, then add the flavored milk, sugar and butter. Bring the mixture to a gentle boil in a broad saucepan over a medium heat, whisking continuously until all the ingredients are well blended. Remove from the heat and whisk until light and fluffy, then spread on the cake. Scatter teaberries over the cake for added eye appeal.

Comments: We prefer a few drops of wintergreen flavoring rather than the additional teaberry candies, because the candy flavor tends to bake out. If the cake is baked in a 9 by 9 by 2-inch (23 by 23 by 5 cm) cake tin, reduce the baking time to about 35 minutes. This same cake batter can also be used for cupcakes and for Whoopie Pies.

Saffron Apeas
Safferich Eepieskuche

As far as we can tell, saffron apeas were well known in the Newmanstown area of Lebanon County, even in the 1870s. After inquiring after a recipe, we were supplied with the one we have adapted here. It came from a descendant of Kate Schaeffer Bennethum (1858-1928), who made this type of apeas for Christmas and birthdays.

Yield: Three 7-inch (18cm) cakes

3 cups (375g) cake flour
½ cup (125g) sugar
1 teaspoon baking soda
1 teaspoon cream of tartar
1 teaspoon salt
2 teaspoons ground coriander
2 teaspoons grated nutmeg
Grated zest of 1 lemon
¼ teaspoon powdered saffron
½ cup (125ml) whole milk
6 tablespoons (90g) unsalted butter
2 large eggs
1½ tablespoons poppy seeds

Preheat the oven to 375F (190C). Grease three 7-inch (18cm) pie pans and set aside. Sift together the pastry flour, sugar, baking soda, cream of tartar, salt, coriander and nutmeg. Add the lemon zest. Dissolve the saffron in the milk, then make a valley in the center of the dry ingredients. Melt the butter and pour this into the valley. Beat the eggs until lemon colored and add the saffron and milk infusion. Pour this into the valley with the butter and work this into a stiff batter. Divide the batter evenly among the three pie dishes and spread smooth with the back of a wet spoon. Scatter the poppy seeds over the pies and bake in the preheated oven for 18 to 20 minutes. Cool on racks. Best served the day they are made. Otherwise, freeze for later use.

sell to outsiders, especially with a side of strawberries and ice cream. Just the same, it is a delightful localism and one more way to enjoy your apeas.

Yield: Three 7-inch (18cm) cakes

3 cups (375g) cake flour
1 cup (250g) vanilla sugar (see note)
2 tablespoons baking powder
½ teaspoon salt
6 tablespoons (90g) unsalted butter
2 eggs
1½ cups (375ml) sour cream

Topping:
3 tablespoons vanilla sugar, one tablespoon
   for each pie

Grease the pie dishes and set aside. Preheat the oven to 375F (190C). Sift together flour, sugar, baking powder and salt. Make a valley in the center of the dry ingredients. Melt the butter and pour it into the valley. Beat the eggs until lemon colored and combine with the sour cream. Pour this into the valley and, using a fork, work the mixture into sticky dough. Divide into 3 equal parts and place them on the prepared pie pans. Spread smooth and even the edges with the back of a wet spoon. Scatter the vanilla sugar evenly over the cakes. Bake in the preheated over for 25 to 30 minutes or until fully puffed and set in the middle. Cool on racks.

Note: You can make your own vanilla sugar by mixing 2 tablespoons (30ml) of vanilla extract with 1 cup (250g) sugar. Stir together with a fork and let it dry before sifting.

Vanilla Apeas
Wanille Eepies

We found this recipe at a Slatington American Legion bake sale, and after inquiring in the area, discovered that the Pennsylvania Dutch in the region north of Allentown have been making vanilla apeas since at least the 1920s. The cake even appeared on the menus of a number of hotels and tearooms farther north, including the Delaware House at Dingman's Ferry and the Hollyhock Tea Room at Bushkill, in the Poconos. It may be that the vanilla flavor was an easy

Yeast-Raised Plum Cake
Blaumekuche

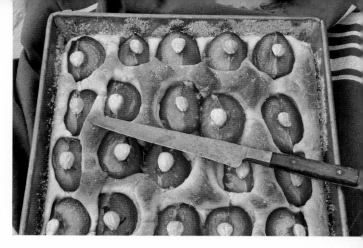

The original recipe below traces to Emma Boller (1859-1934), wife of Martin H. Brumbaugh of Williamsburg in Morrison's Cove, Blair County, Pennsylvania. Martin's father, David Brumbaugh, was well-known in the area for the fine orchard of German prune plums that he sold in markets up and down the Juniata Valley. We found a similar recipe from Lebanon County using sliced peaches, another from Gettysburg using apricots and yet another calling for Seckel pears. The basic idea (cake covered with fresh fruit) is encapsulated in the recipe for Dutch Apple Cake (page 39), which may be considered a short-cut version of this recipe, since it eliminates setting a sponge with yeast. No matter what the baking powder manufacturers may claim, the unique texture of old-style yeast-raised cakes cannot be reproduced with chemicals. This cake is living proof of that happy truism.

Yield: Serves 8 to 10

½ **ounce (15g) dry active yeast**
²/₃ **cup (160ml) lukewarm milk**
7 ounces (220g) unsalted butter
4 tablespoons (60g) superfine sugar (also called caster sugar)
3 large eggs
3 egg yolks
2²/₃ cups (340g) bread flour
Breadcrumbs
8 small prune plums, cut in half and pitted or 16 quarters, depending on the size and shape of the plums
16 whole blanched almonds

Topping:
1 tablespoon (15g) sugar
¼ teaspoon ground cinnamon

Proof the yeast in the milk. While the yeast is proofing, cream the butter and sugar until light and fluffy. Beat the eggs until frothy and lemon colored and combine them with the butter and sugar. Once the yeast is foaming vigorously, add it to the egg mixture and sift in all the flour to form a soft batter. Beat vigorously until the batter becomes slightly stiff and ropey. Cover and set aside in a warm place to double in bulk (this may take 2 to 3 hours). While the batter is proofing, grease a cake pan measuring 10 by 10 by 2 inches (23 by 23 by 5 cm) and dust it liberally with breadcrumbs. Set aside.

Once the batter has doubled in bulk, preheat the oven to 350F (180 C). Stir down the batter and pour it into the prepared cake pan, making certain that the batter is spread evenly into all the corners. Take the sliced plums and press them at even intervals, skin side down, into the batter. Place a blanched almond in each plum where the pit had been. Let the cake recover in a warm place for about 25 minutes, then put it in the preheated oven and bake for 40 to 45 minutes or until the cake taps hollow. As soon as you remove the cake from the oven, scatter a mixture of sugar and cinnamon over the top. Do not cut the cake until it has cooled to room temperature.

THREE

COOKIES AND SMALL PASTRIES

Kichelche un Gleenegebeck

This chapter may be styled in Pennsylfaantisch dialect as *en Luschtkarrebs* (a basket of goodies), because it contains a cornucopia of pastries for all sorts of farmhouse parties. There are gingerbreads, jumbles, lemon hearts, crispy sugar cookies, Lepp cakes (honey cakes), the original Snickerdoodles – even wild chestnut cookies and a variety of roll-outs for the holidays. Like Springerle and New Year's Cake, some require special molds, others only fancy tin cutters; if you are hard pressed to find either, we have supplied the contact information on page 173 for the Foose Tinsmithing Company in Fleetwood, Pennsylvania; they offer an amazing array of handmade cookie cutters online and will also design shapes on commission.

While gingerbread baking is still a highly specialized professional trade in German speaking countries, with many technical baking secrets (not to mention that one must apprentice to become a certified gingerbread baker), the Pennsylvania Dutch situation was never as complicated. There was no guild system to regulate it. Just the same, professionally baked Pennsylvania Dutch gingerbread achieved its own special flavor and texture, because it was made with a *Fordeeg* (foundation dough) created from boiled honey and spelt flour. This was often aged two to three months in advance of final baking. The dough was also subjected to "breaking" (vigorous beating) every two weeks or so in order to tenderize it by breaking down the gluten and thus creating a distinctive spongy texture. A picture of a traditional break bat is illustrated in the glossary on page 164. Homemade gingerbreads were simpler, and some families even dispensed with

spices altogether, figuring that the honey was good enough by itself. Yet in the Dutch Country, there were also many different local ways to spice gingerbreads as well as techniques for glazing them when they came out of the oven. The most traditional way of decorating gingerbreads uses almonds and hazelnuts. The two basic gingerbread spice mixtures used by the Dutch bakeries in Reading, Lancaster, Lebanon, Pottsville, Allentown and York consisted of cinnamon, star-anise, anise and cloves, or cinnamon, star-anise, cloves, coriander and ginger. The spicing was toned back if the main flavoring was nuts, lest the spices upstage them. Some iced gingerbreads were also ornamented with marzipan.

In the past, Pennsylvania Dutch cookies were not found exclusively in the Dutch Country: we would like to point out that the famous crullers, gingerbread boys, brown sugar cookies, oatmeal "muffins" (actually mini-*Datsch* cakes) and small maple-walnut cakes were served at the legendary Fifth Avenue tea room in New York called Mary Elizabeth, and all of those recipes came from Berks County. Founder Mary Elizabeth Evans was the granddaughter of Judge Henry Riegel of Syracuse, New York; his Riegel clan originally came from Pennsylvania, and they were keenly aware of their upper-class Pennsylvania Dutch heritage.

After her 1920 marriage to millionaire Henry D. Sharpe, Mary Elizabeth gradually stepped back from her tea room empire in favor of her sister Martha Evans Stringer (1889-1971), who with her husband, Carlton, became close friends of New York advertising mogul J. George Fredrick. Frederick grew up in Reading, Pennsylvania and was proud of his Pennsylvania Dutch ancestry. He published *The Pennsylvania Dutch and Their Cookery* in 1935 – the first nationally marketed Pennsylvania Dutch cookbook – but more importantly, he reminded Martha Stringer of her Pennsylvania heritage and supplied her with many recipes for the tea room menu. He even mentioned her in his cookbook.

Today, there is a loud chorus of former Mary Elizabeth patrons who consider the tea room and its unique food epiphanous in terms of their culinary coming of age. After Mary Elizabeth Sharpe sold the restaurant in the 1930s and turned her attention to social life in Providence, Rhode Island, her signature recipes underwent many alterations until the time the restaurant closed in 1985 (the same year she died at the ripe age of 100). Just the same, our crullers, sugar *Kringle*, Bellylaps and drop *Kuche* ought to do credit to J. George Frederick and his efforts to elevate the best of the Dutch Country to that former high altar of home-style cooking on Fifth Avenue at 37th.

Adam and Eve Cookies

Adam un Eva Kicherlche

Adam and Eve Day is December 24th, the one day of the year when it was considered bad luck to eat apples. In the eighteenth and nineteenth centuries, when the Dutch normally spent Christmas Eve in church, Adam and Eve Day held special significance since the religious imagery played well with the story of Christmas. The tree depicted in the center of the cookies baked for this occasion was generally equated with the Tree of Life, and was by association an emblem of the Christmas tree. Images of Adam and Eve abound in Pennsylvania Dutch folk art, and several printers issued beautifully colored broadsides with short poems narrating the Adam and Eve story. As for the Adam and Eve cookies, they were given out in church to those children who had excelled that year in school or Sunday school, a culinary reward also intended as moralizing religious instruction.

Yield: 8 to 9 dozen 3-inch (7.5cm) cookies

6 cups (750g) pastry flour
1 cup (125g) finely ground hazelnuts
2 teaspoons baking powder
1 teaspoon salt
1½ tablespoons ground ginger
1½ tablespoons ground anise
1 tablespoon ground coriander
1 cup (250g) sugar
1½ cups (375ml) honey
8 ounces (250g) unsalted butter

Sift together the flour, ground hazelnuts, baking powder, salt and spices. Heat the sugar, honey and butter in a saucepan over a low heat and warm the ingredients until the butter is melted and the sugar is fully dissolved. Cool to room temperature. Make a valley in the center of the dry ingredients, add the honey mixture and combine to form stiff dough. Cover and

ripen in the refrigerator at least 8 hours before using.

Roll out the dough ¼-inch (6mm) thick, then press it into lightly oiled wooden molds. Turn out the shapes, trim and set them on greased baking sheets to dry overnight. The next day, preheat the oven to 325F (165C). Bake in the preheated oven according to size: for small cookies, allow 12 to15 minutes; for large shapes like the Adam and Eve mold (pictured) allow 15 to 20 minutes. Cool on racks.

Pictorial cookies "printed" with carved wooden molds can be further ornamented with colored icing or given a milk and egg yolk wash before baking.

Observation: It is important to allow the cookies time to dry before baking, the same step required when making Springerle (page 83). This will prevent the imprinted design from puffing and distorting in the oven. Large figures like Adam and Eve should be baked on baking parchment and allowed to cool and harden on the parchment after leaving the oven. Depending on the size of the cookie, baking time may run 2 to 3 minutes longer on parchment. Due to the large amount of honey, these cookies will remain soft and pliant and thus not well adapted to decorating with colored icing.

Adam and Eve Cookies

Apeas Drop Cookies
Anis Bleetsche

Pennsylvania Dutch children knew that Christmas was not far off when the anise-flavored drop cookies began to turn up in the farm markets and bake shops. They were standard fare throughout the nineteenth century, and some local bakeries still offered them well into the 1950s. With the renewal of interest in traditional cookery, we decided that this light, puffy classic deserved a fresh place on the holiday menu, especially since the Apeas Drop Cookie is the grandmother of all the apeas cakes now baked in Pennsylvania.

Yield: Approximately 4 to 5 dozen 2-inch (5cm) cookies

2¼ cups (280g) double-sifted pastry flour
2 teaspoons baking powder
1 teaspoon salt
1 cup (250g) caster sugar (also called bar sugar)
4 large eggs, yolks and whites separated
1 tablespoon anise seed

Sift together the flour, baking powder and salt. Set aside. Cream the sugar and egg yolks in an electric mixer until light and fluffy (about 15 minutes to 30 minutes if done by hand). Add the anise seed and sift in half of the flour. Work this into a thick, sticky batter. Beat the egg whites until stiff and forming peaks, then fold them into the batter, alternately sifting in the remaining flour. Beat gently until smooth. Cover and set away in the refrigerator to ripen for 5 hours.

Once the batter has ripened, preheat the oven to 325F (165C). Grease your baking sheets and then place evenly spaced teaspoon-size scoops of cold batter on each, allowing at least 3 inches (7.5cm) between each scoop. Bake in the preheated oven for 12 minutes or until pale golden on the bottom. Cool on racks and store in airtight containers.

Observation: In order to make the cookies as light and airy as possible, it is important that your flour be double sifted before you measure it for the recipe.

Antler Cookies
Haerschhanner

Several Pennsylvania Dutch plain sects still observe Old Christmas (January 6), which is linked on their religious calendars to Old Fastnacht, the Monday before Shrove Tuesday. Old Fastnacht, known as *Haerschmundaag* (Stag's Monday), was never an officially recognized holiday. Some church fathers even discouraged it because it was a day of sacrilegious tricks and shenanigans carried out mostly by children – or as some claimed, by the Waldmops, a mischievous but friendly dwarf who lived in the woods. Families who observed the day treated it like Sunday and set aside all manner of work except for the production of fat cakes for Fastnacht proper, *Haerschkuche* (stag-shaped cookies), and of course the preparation of the "antlers" to go with them.

Antler cookies have come down to us in two distinct forms. Some farmhouse cooks simply appropriated pieces of dough leftover from Fastnachts and used a very sharp knife to cut out antler shapes, which were then deep-fried like fritters. Dusted with powdered sugar, they can hold their own against any New Orleans beignet. Other households prepared special dough similar to shortbread, as in the recipe below. The basic idea was to create a cookie shaped like the antler of a buck, because this was thought to bring about good luck, just as the yellow cornmeal was considered a symbol of fertility and fruitfulness – not to mention its distinctive flavor.

As noted in the Introduction, it was also customary to leave a few of these antler cookies in the woods for the Waldmops, so that he would remember to watch over the fields and gardens come spring planting.

Yield: Approximately 4 dozen

12 tablespoons (190g) unsalted butter
2 eggs
1 cup (250g) sugar
½ teaspoon salt
2 tablespoons (30ml) Kirschwasser (see note)
Grated zest of 1 lemon
1 tablespoon baking powder
2 cups (250g) all-purpose flour
1 cup (125g) fine yellow cornmeal or yellow masa harina

Cream the butter until light and fluffy. In a separate bowl beat the eggs until frothy and combine with the sugar. Once the sugar is fully dissolved, fold this into the butter, then add the salt, Kirschwasser and lemon zest. Sift together the baking powder and both flours, then sift them into the liquid ingredients to form soft dough. Roll into a ball, cover and refrigerate overnight to allow the dough to ripen.

When ready to bake, preheat the oven to 375F (190C). Roll out the dough ½ inch (1.2cm) on a clean surface. Slice the dough into finger-wide pieces about 3 inches (7 cm) long. Cut two diagonal slits into the dough along one side (as pictured) and then spread apart in a slightly curving position to create antler shapes. Put the antlers on ungreased baking sheets and bake in the preheated oven for 12 to 15 minutes, or until the antlers are pale golden on the bottom. Cool on racks and store in airtight containers. Like most shortbreads, these cookies will keep 3 to 4 months.

Note: Some families prefer to heighten the yellow color of the cookies by adding saffron. If you choose to use saffron, dissolve ¼ teaspoon of powdered saffron in the Kirschwasser called for in the recipe. Add the saffron-Kirschwasser as directed.

Bellylaps
Bauchlappe

The recipe for this old-time species of large, flat, molasses cookie came to us from Carrie V. Bitting (1873-1946) of Coopersburg, Pennsylvania. The recipe belonged to her mother, which more or less dates it to the pre-Civil War era. Bellylaps were a particular favorite in country taverns and cake-and-mead shops, since the ingredients were cheap and the cookies could be stored for a long period of time. Bellylaps are still considered one of the Dutch Country classics, because they were also a great favorite with children, who took them to school for lunch and snacking. Furthermore, it was children who gave the cookie its unusual name: *Bauchlappe*

are unsightly folds of fat around the waist, the bane of modern-day dieters and the subject of ridicule back in the days when Yankee lean was an American standard. All the same, bellylap is not the original meaning of the Pennsylvania Dutch name for this cookie. It is a colloquial degeneration of *belziche Leppkuche,* "soft gingerbreads," or more literally: spongy honey cakes. And yes, these cookies should be soft and chewy if they are true to type.

Yield: Approximately 3 dozen 3-inch (7.5cm) cookies

1 egg
½ cup (125ml) barrel molasses
½ cup (125ml) honey (preferably light locust honey)
½ cup (125g) caster sugar (also called bar sugar)
1½ tablespoons (8g) baking powder
3 cups (375g) organic spelt flour
1 tablespoon (5g) ground ginger
2 teaspoons ground coriander
½ teaspoon ground star anise
3 tablespoons (45ml) apple cider vinegar

Beat the egg until lemon colored and frothy. Add the molasses and honey, and beat until smooth and creamy. Gradually sift in the sugar, then sift together the baking powder and 1 cup (125g) of flour and the spices. Sift this into the molasses mixture. Add the vinegar and gradually sift in the remaining flour to create soft dough. Roll the dough into a ball, cover and chill for 2 to 3 hours before baking.

When ready to bake, preheat the oven to 325F (165C). Dust a clean work surface with flour and roll out the dough to ¼-inch (6mm) thick. Using a tin cookie cutter, cut out 2- to 3-inch (5 to 7.5cm) rounds of dough. Lay them on well-greased baking sheets and bake in the preheated oven for 10 to 12 minutes. Bake them "short" (as my great-grandmother used to put it), meaning take them out of the oven just a minute or so early. That way they will be delightfully soft and spongy in the middle. Over-baking will dry them out.

Belschnickel Cookies
Belschnickel Kichelcher

The late Ruth Hershey Irion did much to popularize these cookies during the Pennsylvania Dutch cultural revival in the 1950s. She commissioned copies of antique cookie cutters and sold them through *American Home* magazine, and in 1976, wrote and illustrated a popular children's book called *The Christmas Cookie Tree*. During her heyday, Ruth Irion was considered the reigning queen of Pennsylvania Dutch cookie baking, and her beautifully illustrated portfolio of recipe Fraktur art (Dutch decorated calligraphy) issued in 1947 is now considered a prize collectors item among folk art connoisseurs.

However, it would appear that Mrs. Irion drew her inspiration from *Mary at the Farm*, a now-rare 1916 Pennsylvania Dutch cookbook edited by Edith Thomas. Thomas (who was married to a Quakertown banker) discovered the recipe in northern Bucks County; Thomas explained that the cookies were baked to hand out to the *Belschnicklers* – children and teenagers dressed in outlandish costumes who went mumming from house to house on Second Christmas (December 26). The cookies were distributed much in the same manner as Halloween candies today. The cookie dough is remarkably adaptable and will take elaborate shapes quite readily; thus, they make excellent Christmas tree ornaments. They are also easy to ice or decorate with colored sugar.

12 tablespoons (155g) unsalted butter
1 cup (250g) caster sugar (also called bar sugar)
2 eggs
1 teaspoon vanilla flavoring
1 teaspoon ground cassia
1 teaspoon ground star anise
2 teaspoons baking powder
1 teaspoon salt
3 cups (375g) all-purpose flour
Crystal sugar

Cream the butter until light and fluffy, then add the sugar and whisk vigorously until the sugar is dissolved. Beat the eggs until frothy and lemon colored. Add them and the vanilla to the butter mixture. Sift together the spices, baking powder, salt and flour, then sift and fold this into the wet ingredients. Knead into stiff dough, roll in a ball, cover and chill overnight in the refrigerator. When ready to bake, preheat the oven to 350F (180C) and roll out the dough on a clean surface. Cut out shapes of your choice with fancy tin cutters, scatter crystal sugar over the cookies and bake on well-greased cookie sheets in the preheated oven for 10 to 12 minutes, depending on their size (small cookies will bake more quickly). Cool on racks and store in airtight containers.

The *Belschnickel*

Belschnickel Cookies are also any type of cookie shaped like the *Belschnickel*. His name derives from Pelz Nickolas or "fur-clad Nicholas," yet he was not St. Nicholas; rather, a scary-looking half-man, half-animal who appeared in Pennsylvania Dutch households on Christmas Eve and symbolically punished the bad children with a switching (never applied too vigorously) and then scattered all sorts of Christmas goodies on the floor for the rest of his "terrified" victims. He is depicted in this Swiss cookie mold, dressed in fur, bells hanging from his hat and switch at his side. The book hanging from his waist represents the record book in which he kept track of who was good and who was bad so that he could settle the score each Christmas. He is also holding a small Christmas tree in one hand, one of the earliest eighteenth century depictions of this type of table-top tree, which the Pennsylvania Dutch introduced to mainstream American culture. If you look carefully at the trunk of the tree, you will see a figure of a little man: this is the Waldmops, who is discussed in further detail on page xvi.

Chinquapin Jumbles
Keschde Kringeln

Chinquapins are tiny wild chestnuts with rich, concentrated sweet flavor. They are easy to find in the countryside of rural Pennsylvania, but few people bother to sell them at market due to the work involved in gathering them. This was not the case years ago when they were much favored in game cookery and holiday desserts. Thus, as a substitute, I have used wild American chestnuts, since chestnuts are generally available during the holiday season.

For this recipe, you will need chestnut meal, which you can buy directly from Allen Creek Farm in Ridgefield, Washington (www.Chestnutsonline.com). Or, you can make it yourself if you have a grain mill. The best tasting jumbles will always result from freshly processed chestnuts, which should be roasted in the oven, then removed from their shells and skins. Chop the nuts into small pieces for easier grinding (I use a Corona hand mill), then pass the ground nuts through a fine sieve to achieve the consistency of coarse flour or the best grade of cornmeal. Measure out 2 cups (250g) of meal for the recipe. You can make a marzipan-like confection with the remaining meal; just substitute the chestnuts for ground almonds in any marzipan recipe.

Yield: 4 to 5 dozen

3 large eggs, yolks and whites separated
2 cups (500g) caster sugar (also called bar sugar)
1 cup (250ml) buttermilk
1 tablespoon (15ml) vanilla flavoring
Grated zest of ½ lemon
4 cups (500g) pastry flour
1 tablespoon baking powder
½ teaspoon salt

2 cups (250g) ground wild chinquapins or American chestnuts
Confectioner's sugar (10X)
Beaten egg white
Coarsely chopped and sifted chestnuts

Beat the egg yolks until lemon colored and frothy. Add the sugar and beat until fully dissolved and creamy. Add the buttermilk and vanilla, then the lemon. Sift together the pastry flour, baking powder and salt, and sift this into the ground chestnuts. Fold this into the egg mixture to form loose crumbs. Beat the egg whites until stiff and forming peaks, then fold them into the crumbs to form soft, sticky dough. Cover and set aside in the refrigerator to ripen overnight.

The next day, preheat the oven to 325F (165C). Dust a clean work surface with confectioner's sugar and roll the cold dough into long ropes about ½ inch (1cm) in diameter. Cut the ropes into 4-inch (10cm) lengths and join the ends together to form rings. Line ungreased baking sheets with baking parchment. Arrange the rings evenly spaced on the parchment, allowing for room to spread. Beat the egg white until frothy and forming peaks; brush this over the surface of the cookies and scatter the chopped chestnuts over them. Bake in the preheated oven for 20 minutes or until golden brown on the bottom. Cool on racks and then store in airtight containers.

Crullers
Krollkuche

The term cruller derives from *krollen*, which means to roll; specifically, to roll the fritters in sugar while they are still hot from the kettle. Crullers were popular during the holidays but also sold in vast quantities at county fairs and public events; they were even sold by street vendors. The most common method was to cut the dough into strips with a pastry cutter, giving the edges a jagged pattern. But some cooks went further by creating a myriad of impressive shapes using tin cutters or the tiny cutters used for making vegetable ornaments. Our recipe has been adapted from the manuscript cookbook of Stella Siegfried, who was head cook during the 1870s and 1880s at the Bath Hotel in Bath, Pennsylvania. According to an annotation at the end of the recipe, she acquired it from a Mrs. Moser.

Yield: 2 to 3 dozen, depending on size and shape

8 tablespoons (125g) unsalted butter
2 eggs
¾ cup (185g) sugar
¼ teaspoon salt
½ cup (125ml) sour cream or buttermilk
2 teaspoons baking powder
4 cups (500g) pastry flour

Cream the butter in a large work bowl. In a separate work bowl, beat the eggs until lemon colored and frothy, then add the sugar and salt and beat until the sugar is fully dissolved. Add this to the creamed butter, then add the sour cream. Sift together the baking powder and flour, then gradually sift and fold this into the liquid ingredients to form soft dough. Cover and chill in the refrigerator 2 hours.

When you are ready to cook, heat oil in a deep fryer to 375F (190C). While the oil is heating, roll out the dough ½-inch (1.2cm) thick. Cut it into fancy shapes, like those shown on the facing page. Slide the crullers into the hot oil with a slotted spoon and fry 1 to 2 minutes or until golden brown. Remove with a slotted spoon or wire dipper and drain on absorbent paper. Roll in sugar while still hot or dust with confectioner's sugar once cool.

Finger Dumplings
Finger Gnepp

The Pennsylvania Dutch have invented quite a few desserts that do not fall neatly into any traditional category. Finger Dumplings aren't dumplings, they aren't cakes, and they certainly are not cookies. But since they are small and delicate *(Gleenegebeck)*, we have placed them here. They remind us of the days when baked desserts like this were once common in the homes of the well-to-do Dutch in Reading and other large towns – they do go well with champagne! On the other hand, their country roots are quite obvious: they are made mostly of potatoes. It should not be surprising that this recipe can be traced to the old Spring Mountain House, a once-grand hotel near Schwenksville in the heartland of the old Pennsylvania Dutch potato belt.

Necessary equipment: one porcelain casserole dish measuring 9 ½ by 12 by 2 inches (24 by 30 by 5 cm).

Yield: 50 to 60 Dumplings (Serves 10 to 12)

1 pound (500 kg) floury potatoes
1 egg plus 2 egg yolks (save the egg whites for Lebanon Rusk, on page 18)
1 cup (125g) pastry flour
1 teaspoon salt
1 teaspoon freshly grated nutmeg
1½ tablespoons (7g) baking powder
¼ cup (65g) sugar
3 tablespoons (45g) unsalted butter

Crullers

Finger Dumplings

Pare and cook the potatoes until tender, then press them through a potato ricer or sieve and set aside to cool. Beat the eggs and yolk until lemon colored and fold them into the cooled potatoes. Sift together the flour, salt, nutmeg and baking powder, then sift this into the potato mixture. Work this into soft dough, cover and let ripen in the refrigerator for at least 2 hours. When ready to bake, preheat the oven to 375F (190C).

Place the dough on a clean work surface well-dusted with flour. Using your hands, roll out the dough to form a long rope about the thickness of the little finger. Cut this into 2-inch (5cm) segments. You should have about 50 to 60 pieces.

Soften the butter and liberally grease your baking dish with it, especially on the bottom. Lay the dumpling segments side by side in neat rows. Bake uncovered in the preheated oven for 30-35 minutes or until fully puffed and turning golden brown. Serve immediately as a side dish with fresh or stewed fruit, whipped cream or simply scattered with sugar. Best when hot from the oven.

Frackville Pretzels and Fastnachts
Frackschteddel Bretzle un die Fastnacht

Frackville Pretzels and Fastnachts are made from the same type of dough. The only difference is in the shape. Frackville Pretzels, which used to be available in several bakeshops in Schuylkill and Columbia counties, are made by rolling out the Fastnacht dough and cutting it into pretzel shapes with a large pretzel-shaped cookie cutter. They are then deep-fried like other beignets. In Germany, these pretzel-shaped fat cakes are called *Berliners*.

Fastnachts are probably the best known of all Pennsylvania Dutch fried cakes, since their popularity is regional and no longer just a custom among the Dutch. Fastnacht is Fat Tuesday – Carnival or Mardi Gras to other folks – and the fat cakes made

for this occasion borrow their name from the name of the day. Otherwise, they look like the same kind of beignets made in New Orleans or France, except that for the most part, Fastnachts are made square with no hole in the middle. We prefer to slit them, because that increases the likelihood that they will fry evenly in the center. Badly made Fastnachts are often raw in the middle, a sad result to be avoided. Fastnachts were traditionally made on Old Fastnacht, the day before Fat Tuesday, and some families used the same dough to make Antlers (recipe on page 60).

1 tablespoon dry active yeast
3 cups (750ml) lukewarm whole milk (98F/37C)
8 cups (1 kilo) bread flour
8 tablespoons (125g) unsalted butter
2 eggs
¼ cup (65ml) honey
Sugar and ground cinnamon

Proof the yeast in the milk. Once it is actively foaming, sift in 4 cups (500g) of flour to form batter. Let this rise overnight in a warm place. The next day, cream the butter. In a separate work bowl, beat the eggs until light and lemon colored, then combine them with the honey. Add this to the creamed butter and work the mixture into the raised batter. Sift in the remaining flour into the proofed mixture and knead into soft dough on a well-floured work surface. Cover and let this rise until double in bulk, then knock down and roll out on a clean, well-floured work surface. Cut into Fastnachts or Frackville Pretzels, cover and set aside to rise again.

Once the Fastnachts are risen, carefully slip them into boiling oil brought to a temperature of 375F (190C). Fry a minute or two until golden brown – you may want to try a test run, since frying time will depend on shape and size. Once the Fastnachts are fried, remove from the oil and drain on absorbent paper. Dust liberally with sugar flavored with ground cinnamon.

Observation: Handmade Frackville Pretzel cutters are available from Amish craftsman Reuben E. Mast of Fresno, Ohio. See his listing on page 174. Mast's cutters are marketed as cutters for soft pretzels.

Honey Cakes
Leppkuche

This classic recipe was given to me many years ago by the late Hattie Brunner of Reinholds, Pennsylvania. Hattie was a remarkable cook and a legendary antique dealer with an eye for the unusual. Her equally famous mother-in-law, Hattie Klapp Brunner, also an antique dealer and owner of the once well-known Tulip Shop, obtained the recipe from the old Fox & Ottmeyer bakery in York, Pennsylvania. This was the bakery's once-popular Leppkuche, which at Christmas time during the early 1900s they delivered house to house in horse-drawn wagons. The recipe is best adapted to making round mushroom cap-shaped cookies, the ideal size being 2 inches (5cm) in diameter. Thus, they are specially suited for baking on wafers rather than cutting into fancy shapes. For fancy shapes and dough suitable for carved wooden molds, use the recipe for Adam and Eve Cookies on page 57.

Yield: Approximately 2 dozen

1 cup (250ml) dark honey, preferably
  buckwheat honey
2 tablespoons (30g) unsalted butter
1½ cups (190g) spelt flour
1 cup (125g) rye flour
2 teaspoons baking powder
½ teaspoon salt
2 teaspoons ground coriander
2 teaspoons ground ginger
1 teaspoon ground cinnamon
1 teaspoon ground star anis
¼ teaspoon ground cloves
1 egg yolk (reserve the white for icing)
¼ cup (65ml) buttermilk or sour cream
Grated zest of lemon or orange, optional
Baking wafers (see note)

Warm the honey over a low heat and melt the butter in it. Set aside to cool. Sift together the flours, baking powder, salt and spices. When the honey has cooled, beat the egg yolk and buttermilk and add this to the honey, then sift in the dry ingredients to form soft dough. Add lemon or orange zest if you prefer. Cover and chill 2 days in the refrigerator. If you are the patient type and want truly tender cookies, ripen the dough 3 months in the refrigerator, "breaking" it with a bat twice a week (see the illustration on page 164).

When ready to bake, preheat the oven to 325F (165C) and roll out the dough about ½-inch (2.5cm) thick. Keep it cold; otherwise, it will become sticky. Cut into round 2-inch (5cm) cookies and lay them on baking wafers on ungreased baking sheets. Bake in the preheated oven for 12 to 15 minutes. Once cool, the cookies may be decorated with pink or white ornamental icing (or a combination of both). For fancier cookies, you can experiment with icings flavored with bitter chocolate, mocha or even saffron. You can also ornament them with marzipan figures.

Note: Baking wafers are readily available over the Internet as well as from Echo Hill, listed among the shopping sources on page 173. If you do not have wafers, use baking parchment. Lacking that, simply grease your baking sheets very lightly and proceed from there.

Lemon Hearts

Heart-shaped cookies are made all year around by the Pennsylvania Dutch, so it was not surprising to find these hearts for sale alongside watermelons at a Dauphin County vegetable stand one hot, hot day in July. These cookies have to be one of the best of their kind in the Dutch Country, and I thank Lida Hershberger for sharing her family recipe, which she wrote down from memory on the backside of an old shopping bag. As far as culinary forensics go, this recipe is better if you stick to small hearts as opposed to large.

Yield: 2 to 3 dozen (depends on size of hearts)

8 tablespoons (125g) unsalted butter
1 cup (250g) sugar
2 eggs
1 tablespoon buttermilk
1 teaspoon lemon flavoring or the grated zest of 2 lemons
2 teaspoons baking powder
1½ cups (185g) pastry flour
1 egg white
Lemon sugar (yellow sugar flavored with lemon)

Cream the butter and sugar, then beat the eggs until frothy and lemon colored. Add the buttermilk and flavoring. Combine this with the creamed butter and sugar. Sift together the baking powder and flour, then sift this into the wet ingredients. Work into soft dough, roll into a ball, cover and refrigerate for 3 to 4 hours to allow the dough to ripen.

  When ready to bake, preheat the oven to 350F (180C). Roll out on a clean surface well-dusted with pastry flour. The cold dough should be rolled out to ¼-inch (6mm) thick. Cut out heart shapes with a tin cutter and lay them on lightly greased baking sheets. Beat the egg white until stiff and forming peaks, then brush the cookies with this. Scatter lemon sugar liberally over the cookies. Bake in the preheated oven for 15 minutes or until puffed and golden on the bottom. Cool on racks, then store in airtight containers.

New Year's Cake
Neijohrs Kuche

Many years ago, a small group of Pennsylvania Dutch folk artists held an annual show in an old school at Stouchsburg, Pennsylvania. Ladies from nearby Christ Lutheran Church would sell refreshments, and the whole affair was so popular that people would come from out of state to attend. One of the Lutheran ladies was Annie Nagle (1897-1981), who was considered something of a local personality, not to mention the leading cook in her church. I was there the time she made New Year's Cakes. This is her recipe.

Annie did not bake these cookies often because of the work involved, and not having a wooden mold to stamp them, she did not think they looked right plain. But on this occasion, one of the artists loaned her an old butter print, so with the help of a couple of friends, she turned out a huge batch of cookies stamped with the image of a swan. The secret to good New Year's Cakes is in the dough, which in this case resembles shortbread. The cookies are not overly sweet (a plus) and the addition of caraway seed is always considered a must. While the cookies were normally made for Christmas and New Year's, they stored well and supplied the household with snacks throughout the winter and well into spring. They were even crumbled up to make cracker pies (recipe on page xx).

Cast iron New Year's cookie mold, 1860s

New Year's Cake and Nuttle Cookies

Yield: Approximately 2 dozen, depending on the size of the mold

3½ cups (435g) pastry flour
1 cup (250g) caster sugar (also called bar sugar)
1 tablespoon ground caraway
1 tablespoon ground coriander
4 tablespoons (60g) unsalted butter
4 tablespoons (60g) lard, duck or chicken fat
2 teaspoons caraway seeds
Approximately 1 cup (250ml) cold dry white wine

Sift together the flour, sugar, ground caraway and coriander, then work in the butter and lard to form fine crumbs. Add the caraway seeds and only enough wine to make soft, sticky dough. Dust a clean work surface with pastry flour and knead the dough until it no longer sticks to the hands. Cover and set aside to ripen in a refrigerator for at least 2 hours.

Preheat the oven to 350 F (180C). Roll out the dough ½-inch (1.25cm) thick and cut into squares, rounds or whatever shape best suits your mold. Print the picture on the dough (same process as Springerle cookies) and then place the cookies on lightly greased baking sheets. Bake in the preheated oven for 12 to 15 minutes or until pale golden brown on the bottoms. Cool on racks, then store in airtight containers until needed.

Nuttle Cookies

Nuttle Cookies
Gnuttelkuche

This recipe first came to my attention while interviewing the late Isaac Clarence Kulp (1938-2007), who devoted much of his life to the study of Pennsylvania Dutch culture in his native Montgomery County. The recipe came down from his grandmother on the Kulp side, and while the cookie's name is considered humorous in Dutch (it literally means "horse droppings"), the flavor is special. The cookie is best described as a type of gingerbread using traditional ingredients like spelt and rye. The flavor improves with age, so make them several weeks in advance of when you need them.

Yield: Approximately 4 dozen

4 cups (500g) spelt flour
2 cups (250g) rye flour
1 tablespoon (5g) baking powder
1 teaspoon salt
1 tablespoon (5g) ground cinnamon
1 tablespoon ground (5g) star anise
1 tablespoon (5g) ground ginger
1½ cups (185g) coarsely ground toasted hazelnuts (hazelnut flour)
²/₃ cup (125g) dark brown sugar
1 cup (250ml) buckwheat honey
2 large eggs
1 cup (250ml) sour cream or buttermilk
Powdered chocolate

Sift together the flours, baking powder, salt and spices. Add the nuts. Heat a saucepan and dissolve the sugar in the honey. Once the sugar is completely dissolved, set aside to cool. When the mixture is lukewarm, make a valley in the dry ingredients and add the honey mixture. Beat the eggs until frothy and lemon colored, then add the sour cream. Pour this into the valley with the honey and stir to create soft, sticky dough. Dust a clean work surface with spelt flour and knead the dough with your hands until it no longer sticks to the fingers – from time to time, dust the hands with flour. Form into a ball, cover and refrigerate for 3 to 4 hours or overnight.

When you are ready to bake, preheat the oven to 350F (180C). Break off pieces of dough and roll into 1½-inch (4 cm) balls. Set the balls on greased baking sheets and bake in the preheated oven for 15 to 20 minutes or until puffy and turning golden brown on the bottoms. Cool on racks. When cool, roll the cookies in powdered chocolate and store in airtight containers until needed.

Orange Pretzels
Bommerantze Bretzle

The nineteenth-century fascination with this unusual pretzel no doubt traces to the fact that it resembles a lye pretzel in all its golden brownness, and yet it is perhaps one of the best-tasting "cookie" pretzels on the Pennsylvania Dutch table. Traditional salt pretzels were made with spelt flour, but sweet pretzels, which were known generically as "coffee pretzels" among the Dutch, could be made from just about anything, since – as this name implied – they were considered desserts. Coffee pretzels were meant to be eaten with strong coffee or tea (or with wine). They were definitely a festive treat made for entertaining and Christmas, even for hanging on the tree. They were also made for church schools and distributed to the children on special occasions. One of the earliest references to those sorts of gift pretzels was found in a 1773 Lancaster church register.

We were given this recipe some years ago by the late Dr. Daniel Lee Backenstose of Schaefferstown, Pennsylvania, the author of an amusing little treatise on the art of stuffing pig stomachs. His pretzel recipe was said to have come from the old Lebanon

Valley House Hotel in Lebanon, but we have seen orange and even chocolate pretzels advertised in Reading as early as the 1860s. The original directions called for 4-inch (10cm) lengths of dough, which, once twisted, make extremely tiny pretzels. We opted for 10-inch (25cm) lengths, because they are easier to knot and are less likely to run together during baking. The orange sugar that was scattered over the pretzels in the original recipe was flavored "hail" sugar, resembling in appearance the coarse salt scattered on lye pretzels. That kind of flavored sugar is difficult to find these days, so you can flavor hail sugar with sweet orange oil or simply increase the orange flavoring in the pretzels themselves. The precise amount of oil (or extract) will depend on the quality of the product; cheaper brands tend to bake out. For added effect, you can color the sugar and the pretzels orange – orange dough makes them resemble lye pretzels once baked. Alternately, dip them in orange icing and scatter hail sugar over them before the icing dries.

Yield: 24 to 26 3-inch (7.5cm) pretzels

2 cups (250g) pastry flour
½ cup (125g) caster sugar (also called bar sugar)
1 teaspoon baking powder
4 ounces (125g) cold, unsalted butter
4 tablespoons (35g) finely minced candied orange rind
2 tablespoons freshly grated orange zest
4 large egg yolks
5 to 6 drops sweet orange oil (optional)
Yellow and red food coloring to create orange coloring (optional)
1 egg white
Coarse sugar or hail sugar, preferably orange flavored

Sift together the flour, sugar and baking powder. Rub in the butter to form fine crumbs, then add the minced orange rind and orange zest. In a separate work bowl, beat the egg yolks until light and frothy; add the orange oil (or extract) if you want to intensify the orange flavor – as well as optional coloring (a mix of red and yellow). Combine this with the dry ingredients, then dust a clean work surface with flour. Knead until the dough is no longer sticky. Roll into a ball, cover and refrigerate overnight.

Preheat the oven to 325F (165C). Grease 2 or 3 baking sheets (depending on size) and set aside. Break off a piece of cold dough and roll into ¼-inch (6mm) diameter ropes. Cut these into 10-inch (25cm) lengths. While rolling out the ropes of dough, be certain to taper the thickness so that the middle is fatter than the ends, then twist into pretzels. Lay the pretzels on the baking sheets, spacing them at least 1 inch (2.5cm) apart. Beat the egg white lightly, then brush this over the pretzels and scatter with sugar. Bake in the preheated oven for 15 minutes or until crisp and turning pale gold on the bottom. Remove from the oven and transfer the pretzels to racks to cool. When cool, store in airtight containers until needed.

This recipe can also be used to make Loop Kringles *(Schlupp-Kringle)*:

Instead of shaping the dough into pretzels, cut the ropes into 10-inch (25cm) lengths. Join the ends together to make a ring and bake as directed in the pretzel recipe. These can be hung on a Christmas tree with ribbons tied into bows. Some families also hang them on Easter egg trees.

Sand Tarts (Old Style)
Sandkuche

This very thick species of sand tart came to us from Mary Seaman Shenk (1877-1952), who lived in the Grantville area of East Hanover in Dauphin County. Mrs. Shenk called her cookies "Christmas Cakes" and cut them into squares, which is the original shape of old-style sand tarts. Pennsylvania Dutch bakeshops that sold sand tarts normally cut them out with the same kind of sharp-bladed roller used for gingerbreads. Thus, at the flick of the wrist, a sheet of cookie dough became several dozen sand tarts. Today, many Pennsylvania Dutch cooks like to garnish their sand tarts with half a walnut pressed into the middle. It is de rigueur in Lebanon County to bake them this way. However, we have left ours plain, the way Mrs. Shenk made them.

Yield: Approximately 4 dozen

2 large eggs
2 cups (500g) caster sugar (also called bar sugar)
1 cup (250ml) sour cream
1 cup (250ml) melted butter (or half butter and half lard)
1 tablespoon grated zest of orange or lemon
4 cups (500g) pastry flour
1 tablespoon baking powder
1 tablespoon ground cardamom
Confectioner's sugar for dusting
Coarse crystal sugar for garnishing

Beat the eggs until light and frothy, then cream them together with the sugar. Add the sour cream and gradually beat in the melted butter (it should not be hot). Add the orange zest. Sift together the flour, baking powder and cardamom, then sift this into the batter, folding as you work, to form soft dough. Cover and refrigerate over night.

The next day, preheat the oven to 350F (180C). Dust a clean work surface with Confectioners (10-X) sugar. Break off lumps of cold dough and dust with just enough confectioners (10-X) sugar to keep the surface of the dough dry for handling. Roll out ½-inch (1.25cm) thick. Cut into 2-inch (5cm) squares and then set the cookies on greased baking sheets. Sprinkle liberally with coarse sugar or crystal sugar. Bake in the preheated oven for approximately 15 minutes or until golden on the bottom. Cool on racks and store in airtight containers.

Sand Tarts (top) and Orange Pretzels (bottom)

Snickerdoodles and Snowballs

Snickerdoodles
Schnickerdudle

This is one of those Pennsylvania Dutch cookies with a name that has wandered far from its original meaning. A *Schnickelfritz* is a mischievous child, and *dudle* means to fool around sexually. Thus, in Pennsylvania Dutch, the cookie's name is hardly innocent. That is probably not the intention of all the good Dutch mothers who make these cookies for their kids. As it turns out, snickerdoodle is a corruption of *Schnitt-Nudle*, a pastry traditionally made for All Saints (November 1).

We found the cookies under the name Snip Doodles in a 1905 Reading cookbook, then Snippy Doodles in another. By the 1920s and the growing popularity of Halloween trick-or-treats, *Schnitt-Nudle* evolved into the snickerdoodle we know today. It has lost its connection to Halloween, but many Pennsylvania Dutch make it for birthdays or Christmas. The recipe on page 80 will show you how to make the original *Schnitt-Nudle* as described in an 1859 recipe published many times in the Reading *Adler* (the German edition of the Reading Eagle newspaper). Meanwhile, here is an archetypical snickerdoodle recipe (there are many variations), as supplied to me by a friend of the late Ernie Risser (1956-2014), whose diner near Womelsdorf, Pennsylvania, was considered one of the best for authentic Dutch cooking. Ernie made these cookies as a snack for himself, sometimes sold them over the counter, and sometimes even added saffron to give them what he jokingly referred to as "local color."

Yield: 2½ dozen

8 tablespoons (125g) unsalted butter
¾ cup (185g) sugar
1 teaspoon vanilla flavoring or saffron to taste
1 large egg
1⅓ cups (170g) all-purpose flour
2 teaspoons baking powder
½ teaspoon salt
2 tablespoons (30g) sugar
2 teaspoons ground cinnamon

Cream the butter, sugar and flavoring, then beat the egg until lemon colored and add it to the butter mixture. Sift together the flour, baking powder and salt, and sift this into the wet ingredients and work into dough. Cover and chill 1 to 2 hours so that the dough will ripen.

When ready to bake, preheat the oven to 400F (200C). Break off pieces of dough and roll them into balls about as large as a walnut. Roll the balls in sugar combined with cinnamon and arrange the balls on ungreased cookie sheets, spacing them about 2 inches (5cm) apart. Bake in the preheated oven for 8 to 10 minutes or until light brown. Cool on the baking sheets before removing. Once cool, store in airtight containers.

Lebanon Valley House Hotel, old woodcut, 1870s.

Snowballs
Schneeballe

Our heirloom recipe came to us courtesy of Lenore K. Fitterling of Denver, Pennsylvania, and calls for pecans. While pecans may ring Southern to most ears, they are indeed a close relative of our local hickory nuts. Pecans are botanical imports from outside our borders, and the trees do thrive in parts of the Keystone State, so the two nuts may be treated as loosely interchangeable. Perhaps it would also be appropriate to point out that there was a pecan craze in the Dutch Country in the early 1900s. The Keystone Pecan Research Laboratory at Manheim, Pennsylvania, issued a pecan cookbook in 1925 called *800 Proved Pecan Recipes*, which included a recipe for a steamed (no less!) snowball pudding strewn in its fresh steaminess with chopped pecans. This is not the snowball of tradition, nor of Mrs. Fitterling's popular cookie, but then again, in Pennsylvania Dutch cookery, many things are called snowballs. There are fried balls of cake similar to Boskie Boys (page 151) that are rolled in powdered sugar like doughnuts, and there are baked cookie balls rolled in shredded coconut. Mrs. Fitterling's comes closest to the snowball recipes preserved in old German cookbooks, a confection that easily dates to the late Middle Ages, leaving aside the pecans of course.

Yield: Approximately 3 dozen

8 ounces (250g) unsalted butter
¼ teaspoon salt
1 teaspoon vanilla flavoring
½ cup (90g) confectioner's sugar
2½ cups (310g) pastry flour
¾ cup (90g) finely chopped pecans or hickory nuts

Cream the butter, then add the salt, vanilla and sugar. Beat vigorously until smooth, and sift in the flour. Add the nuts, cover and chill in the refrigerator about 2 hours to ripen. When ready to bake, roll the dough into small 1½-inch (4cm) diameter balls. Line baking sheets with baking parchment and place the balls on them about 2 inches (5cm) apart. Bake for 15 to 18 minutes or until golden brown on the bottom in an oven preheated to 325F (165C). Then roll immediately in confectioner's sugar. Once the cookies are cool, roll them a second time in confectioner's sugar. Store in airtight containers until needed.

Slit Fritters (Harvest Home Fritters)
Schnitt-Nudle

Slit Fritters are lozenge or diamond-shaped doughnuts that were originally made as festive treats for All Saints (November 1). They were particularly popular among the Swabian element of the Pennsylvania Dutch community and were often given out as part of the refreshments following church services on All Saints. As we have mentioned on page 79, it is this pastry that gave rise to the popular snickerdoodle, now found in cookbooks all over the United States, even though the two are now quite different from one another, aside from the November 1 connection. The name has even changed in Germany: today, *Schnitt-nudeln* is the commercial term for shredded pasta, strands of hair-like dough.

In a sense, Slit Fritters are the autumnal counterpart to Fastnachts, since they are yeast-raised, fried in fat and represent harvest feasting that in medieval terms ended on November 15th with the beginning of Fall Lent, a period of fasting for 40 days before Christmas. Since Protestantism dropped these traditional Catholic customs, they survived with unofficial sanction in the folk culture of the

Pennsylvania Dutch in the context of what one might call "village culture," as opposed to church-approved observances. All the same, some ministers allowed *Schnitt-Nudle* as part of the Harvest Home festivities, and the power of the ladies' committees was often enough to settle the matter. Ladies' committees are not to be taken lightly: in the Mahantongo Valley of Schuylkill County, a group of determined women sold these diamond-shaped doughnuts at bake sales to raise money for a new church (they paid for it brick by brick).

Yield: Approximately 2 ½ dozen, depending on the size of the diamonds

2 tablespoons dry active yeast
1½ cups (375ml) lukewarm whole milk (98F/37C)
1 large egg
1 egg yolk
2 teaspoons salt
4 cups (500g) bread flour
2 tablespoons sugar
2 teaspoons ground cinnamon (or mace, nutmeg, spice of your choice)

Proof the yeast in milk until actively foaming. Beat the egg and yolk until light and frothy, and combine this with the yeast. Sift together the salt and flour, and add to the yeast mixture. Work into soft, pliant dough on a clean work surface well-dusted with bread flour. Knead until soft and pliant, roll out ½-inch (1.25cm) thick and cut into lozenge (diamond) shapes. Set the Slit Fritters on baking sheets to rise in a warm place about 25 to 30 minutes. Once recovered, fry them in lard or cooking oil preheated to 375F (190C), until they turn golden color. Remove with a slotted spoon and drain on absorbent paper. While still hot, dust with a mixture of sugar and ground cinnamon and serve immediately.

Observation: To avoid raw centers (which sometimes happens when deep-frying fritters) cut a small slit in the center of each diamond. This will ensure that the centers cook evenly, and in any case, this slit gives the fritters their distinctive appearance.

Springerle Cookies
Schpringerkuche

In old-time Pennsylvania Dutch households where baking took special pride of place, the kitchen was inevitably a repository for all sorts of cookie cutters, molds and stamps. Some of them were imported and sold by local bakeries during the Christmas season, but just as many were homemade or produced by manufacturing confectioners like the Fries family of Reading, George Endriss of Philadelphia, and similar firms in large towns throughout the region. Some of the most innovative were the metal springerle molds produced during the 1870s by Endriss in an attempt to launch springerle baking into mass production.

However, you do not need to spend a great deal of money on showcase antique molds; just peruse eBay for springerles and a wide range of choices will pop up. That said, you will need some sort of mold to make springerles; even an old butter print will do. Our recipe has been adapted from an heirloom recipe that came to us from a descendant of Laura Heffner Schoch (1867-1958), the wife of a Shamokin, Pennsylvania, physician. It was given to Mrs. Schoch by her mother, Hannah Good Heffner.

Baking spingerles is an art because it takes trial and error to match the right dough to the right mold. Even the type of wood can make a big difference in the way the cookies take to the print designs. Mrs. Schoch's recipe produces very nice cookies for eating, but the pictures tend to bake out if you roll the dough too thick. If you would prefer the cookies more tender, add 1/3 cup (45g) of potato starch to the dough, enough so that the dough feels like bread dough and does not stick to the hands. If you want rock-hard Springerles with perfect pictures like the ones made in German bakeries, then leave out the baking powder. You can use the hard cookies for Christmas tree decorations – they will keep indefinitely if stored in airtight containers.

Many years ago while visiting the Staib bakery in Ulm, Germany, I observed that these expert bakers were drying their Springerles in the same warm room where they proofed bread, and a fan was circulating air over the surface of the cookies to dry them out prior to baking. Even then, not all the cookies baked picture perfect, but of course, those rejects never made it into the display cases. So, to avoid frustration and disappointment, decide ahead of time what your goal should be: cookies for eating or cookies as decoration. Furthermore, I think that for home cooking, springerle molds depicting four or six pictures with deeply carved uncomplicated designs are the most manageable. This way, it is easier to distribute pressure evenly when imprinting the dough – large molds inevitably create waste with broken or half-printed images around the edges. Modern bakeries do the printing with mechanical rollers; in the old days, a baking apprentice actually stood on the mold. We leave such experimentations to your imagination!

Yield: Approximately 2 to 3 dozen

3 large eggs, separated
1⅓ cups (250g) confectioner's (10-X) sugar
Grated zest of 1 lemon
2 cups (250g) pastry flour
1 teaspoon baking powder
1 tablespoon anise seed or more to taste

Beat the eggs until lemon colored in a deep work bowl, then fold in the sugar and continue to beat until light and frothy. Beat the egg whites until stiff and forming peaks, and fold them into the egg and sugar mixture. Add the lemon zest. Sift the flour and baking powder together twice, and fold in the flour mixture.

Form the dough into a ball and cover. Set in the refrigerator to ripen for at least 10 hours.

To use a springerle mold, first chill it in the refrigerator. Brush it lightly with olive oil, then wipe it dry with a clean cloth. If the mold has an elaborate design, dust it lightly with pastry flour. These precautions will prevent the mold from sticking to the dough.

To make the cookies, roll out the dough ¼-inch (6mm) thick between two sheets of wax paper, preferably on a marble slab in order to keep the dough cold. Put the dough in the freezer and let it chill until firm, but not frozen. Remove from the freezer, dust the surface of the dough with potato starch and then press the chilled mold face down into the dough and gently pull away. Cut out the cookies along the borders of

the designs and set them on clean baking sheets to dry in an unheated room for 3 to 4 days. This drying process hardens the image and prevents the pictures from puffing up as they bake. Ideally, the puffing should go downwards to create a "foot" (raised area) underneath each cookie.

Preheat the oven to 275F (135C). Scatter the anise seeds on lightly greased baking sheets and set the cookies on top. Bake approximately 18 to 20 minutes, or longer, depending on the size of the cookies, or until golden brown on the bottom. Cool on racks and further decorate with colored icings, if desired. Store in airtight containers. These cookies will last several months and improve in flavor over time.

Sugar Cookies (Ritner Roll-Outs)
Ritner Ausdreele

Joseph Ritner (1780-1869) was governor of Pennsylvania from 1835 to 1839, one of several Pennsylvania Dutch governors of the state. Born in Reading, he espoused anti-upper-class politics and became a member of the Anti-Masonic Party. Perhaps more importantly, he was also an outspoken Abolitionist, which earned him great popularity well beyond the borders of Pennsylvania. Why his name became attached to a cookie is still a matter of conjecture, yet it may have something to do with his Abolitionist connections. These popular cookies were served during his funeral at his Cumberland County farm in 1869. The recipe here is half the original proportion.

Yield: Approximately 2 dozen cookies

4 ounces (125g) unsalted butter
1 cup (250g) caster sugar (bar sugar)
2 eggs
½ cup (125ml) buttermilk
2 teaspoons almond flavoring or to taste
2 cups (250g) all-purpose flour
¾ cup (75g) almond flour (finely ground almonds)
½ teaspoon salt
1 tablespoon (5 g) baking powder

Topping:
1 egg white
Vanilla sugar or raw sugar

Cream the butter and sugar until fluffy, then beat the eggs until frothy and lemon colored. Add the buttermilk and almond flavoring. Combine this with the butter mixture. Sift together the flour, almond flour, salt and baking powder in a large mixing bowl, then combine this with the liquid ingredients. Work this into soft, sticky dough, cover and refrigerate for at least 2 hours before using. Then preheat the oven to 350F (180C).

Using a cold rolling pin (preferably glass or marble), roll out the dough on a clean work surface well-dusted with flour until ¼-inch (6mm) thick. Cut out the cookies with a rounded fluted-edge cookie cuter, then cut out a star from the center of each. Place the cookies on a well-greased baking sheet. Beat the egg white until stiff and forming peaks, and brush each cookie with the whites. Scatter sugar over the top and bake in the preheated oven for 15 minutes. Cool on racks.

Watch Point: Since these cookies puff up considerably, space them about 1 inch (2.5cm) apart on the baking sheets.

Sugar Kringles
Zucker Kringle

There are two types of kringles in Pennsylvania Dutch cookery. One is formed into a large loop *(Schlupp-Kringle)*, which old pictures often show as a Christmas tree decoration, and then this one, which is like a sand tart with a hole in the middle. The *Schlupp-Kringle* are light and crispy and similar to pretzels in texture (refer to the recipe on page 76); this version is puffy and somewhat brittle, so use caution when removing them from your baking sheets.

This delightful Christmas recipe came to us courtesy of the late Emma Gable (1880-1980). Her popular cookie was widely circulated in the area around Glen Rock, a village located near the Maryland border in southern York County. Glen Rock is probably better known for its Glen Rock Carolers, who sing Christmas carols in three-part harmony every Christmas Eve. Handing out sugar kringles to the carolers has been part of an annual caroling tradition that began in 1848.

Yield: 18 to 24 3 ½ inch (about 9cm) cookies

1 cup (250g) sugar
8 tablespoons (125g) unsalted butter
3 eggs
½ cup (125ml) sour cream
4 cups (500g) pastry flour
1 tablespoon (5g) baking powder
1 teaspoon salt
2 teaspoons ground cinnamon
1 teaspoon ground ginger
1½ teaspoons ground cardamom
2 egg whites
Coarse sugar

Preheat the oven to 350F (180C). Cream the sugar and butter until light and fluffy. In a separate work bowl, beat the eggs until lemon colored, then combine them with the sour cream. Add this to the creamed sugar and butter.

In a separate work bowl, sift together the flour, soda, and spices twice, then sift this into the batter, folding it in gradually until it forms soft dough. Cover and refrigerate for at least 1 hour. Break off pieces of cold dough and roll out ¼-inch (6mm) thick on a work surface lightly dusted with pastry flour. Cut into 3 ½-inch (about 9cm) rounds with a hole in the center. Lay the cookies on greased baking sheets.

Beat the egg whites until stiff and forming peaks, brush this over the cookies, then scatter them liberally with coarse sugar. Bake in the preheated oven for 15 minutes or until golden on the bottom. Cool on racks and then store in airtight containers.

White Peppernuts
Weisse Peffernisse

There are two kinds of Pennsylvania Dutch peppernuts, white and brown – the latter invariably spiced with black pepper and cardamom. Their color is determined by the type of dough and sugar used. Generally speaking, the brown peppernuts are denser and more like honey cakes in texture; thus, they retain their shape, which is created with a carved mold or with a real walnut shell. The white nuts puff too much to retain a nut-like appearance, but they redeem themselves with real old-time Christmas flavor. Our recipe has been adapted from the original recipe of Lovinia Santee (1831-1909) of Bath, Pennsylvania. She was a friend of Stella Siegfried, cook at the Bath Hotel, whose recipe for crullers may be found on page 66. And lastly, peppernuts of all kinds were the favorite food of the mythic (or not so mythic) *Elbedritsch*, a bird-like creature who inhabits the woods of the Dutch Country. For more on him, read the sidebar. He is depicted here in the sidebar.

Yield: Approximately 4 dozen

3½ cups (400g) organic, whole wheat pastry flour
1¾ cups (400g) caster sugar (also called bar sugar)
2 teaspoons baking powder
1 tablespoon (5g) freshly grated nutmeg
1 tablespoon (5g) ground cinnamon
1 teaspoon ground cardamom
½ teaspoon ground cloves
Grated zest of 1 lemon
½ cup (95g) finely minced candied citron
4 large eggs
5 tablespoons (75ml) sour cream
1 cup (125g) all-purpose flour
Confectioner's sugar (optional)

Sift the pastry flour, sugar, baking powder, nutmeg, cinnamon, cardamom and cloves three times in a large work bowl. Add the lemon zest and citron. Beat the eggs until lemon colored and combine with the sour cream. Make a well in the center of the dry ingredients and pour the egg mixture into it. Stir to form a sticky dough. Knead in the all-purpose flour until the dough no longer sticks to the hands. Form into a ball, cover and set in the refrigerator to ripen for 2 days.

To bake, preheat the oven to 325F (170C). Break off pieces of dough and roll into balls the size of large cherries. Set them on greased baking sheets, allowing ample space for puffing. Bake 12 minutes, then cool on racks. Roll in confectioner's sugar if desired. Store in airtight containers at least 2 weeks before serving: the flavor of the cookies improves with age.

Land of the *Elbedritsch*

The *Elbedritsch* belongs to the world of the Waldmops, and some even claim he is his pet. No one knows for sure whether there is just one *Elbedritsch* as spotted in many different places, or several of these creatures on the loose. There is even a hill in Lancaster County where he or they are supposed to live. What we do know is that the *Elbedritsch* is much easier to spot at night (they are nocturnal) the more whiskey you imbibe. Pennsylvania Dutchmen well into their bottles have been known to send out a colleague in search of the creature with lantern in one hand and a long stick in the other. Of course, the *Elbedritsch* can see him coming, so escape is always a foregone conclusion.

The late Pennsylvania Dutch potter Lester Breiniger made the image of the *Elbedritsch* seen here. When asked how he knew he got it right, he responded  that he was not sure since he had no whiskey in the house, but wearing a wreath of Eyebright in full bloom works just as well. If you are really intent on capturing one of these creatures, then it is important to know that they have a passion for peppernuts and will even reveal the location of buried treasures in return for some of these cookies. Being hard up for cash, we set a trap for the *Elbedritsch* and loaded it with peppernuts. All we managed to capture was a skunk.

Pepper Nuts

1 lb butter 1 lb sug~~ar~~ ... 1 teaspoon full of ...
pearlash soaked in ... of milk, rose watter,
cloves, carraway see... ...ough not very sift

Whoopie Cake
Greischlikuche

While the original Whoopie cakes were chocolate with a vanilla-flavored fondant filling, the variations found in the Dutch Country today are truly ingenious. One of the most popular among the Amish is a red velvet cake adaptation; this reddish-brown chocolate cake was known years ago as Mahogany Cake. Its unique color was caused by a chemical reaction between baking soda and chocolate. Today, red food coloring is added to make the cake part even redder. Rather than go that route, I am using an original 1911 Mahogany Cake recipe given to me by Kate Zug, an Amish housewife who has a cake-and-pie business near Bird-in-Hand, Pennsylvania. When baked in muffin rings, these Whoopies will produce cakes of equal size that are easily sandwiched into "pies."

Yield: Approximately 2 to 3 dozen

Cake Part:
1¼ teaspoon baking soda
1 cup (250ml) strong coffee
½ cup (60g) powdered cocoa
8 tablespoons (125g) unsalted butter
1½ cups (375g) light brown sugar
3 eggs
1 teaspoon vanilla flavoring
1 teaspoon baking powder
2 cups (250g) cake flour

Dissolve the baking soda in 1/2 cup (125ml) of coffee. Bring this to a gentle boil and dissolve the cocoa in it. Stir continuously until the chocolate becomes smooth and creamy. Set aside to cool. Cream the butter and sugar until light and fluffy. Beat the eggs until lemon colored and combine them with the butter mixture. Add the chocolate and the remaining coffee. Sift together the baking powder and flour, then sift this into the wet ingredients. Stir to create a thick batter.

Preheat the oven to 425F (220C). Drop the batter in even spoonfuls on greased cookie sheets or use small muffin rings and fill them with batter. Bake for 7 to 8 minutes, then remove from the oven and cool on racks. Once the cakes are cool, add the filling (see below) and put them together.

Potato Fondant Filling:

Yield: 3 pounds (1½ kg) fondant

1 cup (250g) steamed mashed potatoes
2 egg whites
2½ pounds (1¼ kg) confectioners sugar 10X (about 10 cups)
2 teaspoons vanilla flavoring

Once the potatoes are cool, gently work the egg whites into them – do not beat the mixture! Gradually sift in the sugar until the fondant becomes stiff and no longer adheres to the hands. Flavor with vanilla if you prefer. Place the fondant on a cold marble slab and knead it like bread dough until soft and silky (about 25 to 30 minutes). Cover and store the fondant in the refrigerator until required.

To fill the Whoopie Cakes, roll out on a clean surface and cut into discs the same diameter as the cakes.

Some Whoopie Cake Facts

Are they cakes, pies or cake sandwiches? Probably a little bit of each. Whoopies are an industrial hybrid created in 1926 by the Berwick Cake Company of Roxbury, Massachusetts. They were not invented at Berwick, Maine, in spite of claims to the contrary. In 1988, Allene White interviewed the former employees of the Berwick Cake Company and published what she learned in the *Maine Sunday Telegram*. Eddie O'Reilly, who had worked in the bakery since 1923, saw the whole story unfold. The cakes made today by the name Whoopie or Whoopee are nothing like the originals, because the Berwick Cake Company's high-ratio chocolate cake formula could only be produced with industrial machinery. What we eat today are look-alikes made an entirely different way.

The name of the cake-sandwich is derived from the Broadway musical "Whoopee," which was playing in Boston a few years after the then-nameless cakes were first created. The cake company patented the name Whoopie (slightly different spelling), because it would have been a copyright infringement had the spelling appeared the same as the musical. That patent expired when the bakery went out of business in 1977. It was also during the 1970s that Whoopie cakes entered the Dutch Country via the Amish from the Big Valley of Mifflin County. The cake's popularity got off to a slow start, but once recipes began to appear in Amish publications, especially under the guise of something easy to make for Amish school lunch boxes, the cakes began to appear everywhere the Amish sold baked goods. Now they are one of the most common pastries eaten in the Dutch Country, even though they are not a Pennsylvania Dutch invention. According to the company's last president, the secret to the success of the original Whoopies was in the filling, a special-formula fondant boiled at 240F (116C) and then rolled in a machine to create the desired texture. The closest thing to it is potato fondant, which we prefer to Kate Zug's Marshmallow Fluff, since it is a natural ingredient and does not ooze out of the cakes once they are stuck together.

FOUR

FLATBREADS CALLED DATSCH

Datsch Kuche

*D*atsch represents a baking category all its own, although sharing some similarities with the Italian *foccacia*. Its Pennsylfaanisch name is a dialect term originating from southwest Germany to describe food with mush-like consistency, or flat breads made from mush or porridge. Thus, the root meaning of the Pennsylvania Dutch word *Datschkuche* is "mush cake." Datsch is also interchangeable with *Batsch*, the same word pronounced a slightly different way, which many Pennsylvania Dutch children use for patty cake in a popular dialect word game. It even appears under the name of *Blotch Kuchen* in an Adamstown church cookbook from the 1950s. However, *Datsch* is the oldest form and derives from Latin *dedicatio*, an offering. So the line of thinking among food historians is that this flat bread probably descends from some very ancient form of Rhineland bannock (Johnny cake) with roots in pre-Christian tradition.

Regardless of its age and genealogy, *Datsch* as a distinct branch of baking has been largely ignored in published Pennsylvania Dutch cookbooks, because the old-time breads made with mush or porridge (or more recently with mashed potatoes) were considered poverty foods and not subject to improvement – certainly not the sort of progressive thing worthy of *Good Housekeeping* or *Bon Appétit*. Yet no Dutchman scoffs at mush muffins (cornmeal *Datsch* cakes miniaturized), and few people seem to realize that under various disguises, *Datsch* is still very much with us, although it has evolved into something a bit different from its stodgy ancestor. Furthermore, Dutch cooks began calling the dish by other names when they stopped using the dialect, and this further disconnected them from the root idea. A case in point would be Elizabeth Rahn's recipe for Raisin *Datsch* on page 102; she called it Bethlehem Cake, doubtless because that is where she found the recipe. Just the same, there are two types of *Datsch* cakes, and we have devoted an entire chapter to their rich and seemingly infinite variation – a first for any American cookbook.

Both types were normally eaten with stewed fruit, applesauce – or even stewed vegetables when prepared without sugar. The oldest and most traditional form was raised with yeast and required long, slow baking at a low temperature. This flat bread was brought from the Rhineland to colonial Pennsylvania, where it was baked in iron skillets down hearth under hot ashes, like St. Gertrude's *Datsch* on page 103 (I have modernized that baking technique). The rustic character of this kind of bread declined in popularity with the advent of the cast iron cook stove in the 1840s.

The cook stove and the concurrent introduction of chemical leaveners (such as saleratus) led to the emergence of the other type of *Datsch* following the Civil War, when many Dutch housewives began embracing shortcuts like baking powder, fewer eggs and more adventuresome combinations of ingredients: a case in point, the Peanut *Datsch* on page 98, a late Victorian recipe developed for the Bethany Orphans' Home in Womelsdorf, Pennsylvania. The baking powder *Datsch* is also lighter in texture, oftentimes sweetened with a little sugar, and may be considered an emergency dessert, since it can be assembled and baked within an hour. *Datsch* also makes a respectable coffee cake, which is doubtless one reason it has remained popular in Pennsylvania Dutch farmhouse cookery.

Apple Datsch (Sweet)
Ebbeldatsch (Siesser)

Excellent when served with stewed apples and rhubarb – or stewed gooseberries. If serving with stewed fruit, eliminate the caraway seeds. The apple of choice for this dish was usually some type of codling (cooking apple), like Summer Rambo, a variety that is still common in Pennsylvania farm markets. Lacking an heirloom variety, you can always substitute Granny Smith, although Granny Smith does not break down quite like the old-time cookers.

Yield: Serves 8 to 10

Fine breadcrumbs for dusting
2 cups (250g) all-purpose flour
1 tablespoon baking powder
1 teaspoon salt
½ cup (125g) sugar
1 cup (175g) tart green apples, pared, cored and shredded on the large holes of a vegetable grater
4 tablespoons (65g) melted butter
2 eggs, yolks and whites separated
1 cup (250ml) buttermilk

Topping:
2 tablespoons coarse sugar
1 teaspoon caraway seed or anise seed (or more to taste)

Preheat the oven to 375F (190C). Grease a *Schales* pan and dust this with fine breadcrumbs. Set aside.

Sift together the flour, baking powder, salt and sugar, then add the shredded apple. Stir so that the apples and dry ingredients are thoroughly mixed. Make a valley in the center of the dry ingredients and add the melted butter. Beat the egg yolks until light and frothy, add the butter milk, then pour this into the dry ingredients and whisk until smooth. Beat the egg whites until they form stiff peaks, and fold this into the batter. Pour the batter into the prepared *Schales* pan. Scatter the sugar and caraway seed (or anise) over the top.

Bake in the preheated oven for 25 to 30 minutes or until fully risen and turning golden. Best when hot from the oven or reheated in a microwave oven for 1 minute on high.

Green Tomato and Apple Datsch
Griene Tomaets un Ebbel Datsch

In the fall, when frost begins nipping the air, there is always a scramble in the kitchen garden to salvage whatever lingering fruits and vegetables may be on hand. This is one reason the Pennsylvania Dutch housewife likes her chow-chows: just about anything can go into those pickles. By the same token, firm green tomatoes that otherwise would ripen insipid on a windowsill are perfect for this flavorful autumn dessert.

Yield: Serves 8 to 10

Fine breadcrumbs for dusting
2 cups (250g) all-purpose flour
1 tablespoon baking powder
1 teaspoon salt
½ cup (125g) sugar
½ cup (85g) tart green apples, pared, cored and
  shredded on the large holes of a vegetable grater
½ cup (85g) firm green tomatoes, shredded on the
  large holes of a vegetable grater
Grated zest of 1 lime
1 tablespoon (10g) poppy seeds
1 teaspoon freshly grated ginger
4 tablespoons (65g) melted butter
2 eggs, yolks and whites separated
1 cup (250ml) sour cream

Topping:
Poppy seeds

Preheat the oven to 375F (190C). Grease a *Schales* pan and dust this with fine breadcrumbs. Set aside.

Sift together the flour, baking powder, salt and sugar, then add the shredded apple, shredded green tomato, lime zest, poppy seeds and grated ginger. Stir so that the ingredients are thoroughly mixed. Make a valley in the center of the flour mixture and add the melted butter. Beat the egg yolks until light and frothy, add the butter milk, then pour this into the dry ingredients and whisk until smooth. Beat the egg whites until they form stiff peaks, and fold this into the batter. Pour the batter into the prepared *Schales* pan. Scatter poppy seeds over the top.

Bake in the preheated oven for 25 to 30 minutes or until fully risen and turning golden. Best when served at room temperature.

Hickory Nut Dasch, Oatmeal Datsch
and Raisin Datsch

Hickory Nut Datsch
Hickernuss Datsch

This recipe conforms very neatly to the traditional meaning of *Datsch*, because it starts out as cornmeal mush and then evolves into flat bread of a truly unique texture. If you prefer it a little sweeter, you can double the amount of sugar in the batter. However, the predominant flavor should be hickory nuts, one of the most popular native nuts in Pennsylvania Dutch cookery.

The white cornmeal that we used for this recipe was hand ground from Iroquois Tooth Corn (also called Gourd Seed Corn). This once-popular heirloom corn was widely planted in the Dutch Country throughout much of the nineteenth century. You can purchase seed for this rare variety online from the Roughwood Seed Collection (www.RoughwoodSeeds.org). If there is enough demand, one of the Collection's farmers will grow enough for sale as cornmeal or make arrangements for special orders.

Yield: Serves 8 to 10

Fine breadcrumbs for dusting
2 cups (300g) semolina
1 tablespoon baking powder
¼ cup (65g) sugar
1 teaspoon salt
1½ cups (150g) finely chopped hickory nuts
   (oatmeal consistency)
Grated zest of 1 lemon
1 cup (225g) cooked cornmeal mush
   (see Watch Point below)
4 tablespoons (65g) melted unsalted butter
2 eggs, yolks and whites separated
1 cup (250ml) sour cream or buttermilk

Topping:
Chopped hickory nuts
2 tablespoons (30g) sugar (optional)

Preheat the oven to 375F (190C). Grease a *Schales* pan and dust it with breadcrumbs. Set aside.

Sift the semolina, baking powder, sugar and salt into a deep work bowl. Add 1 cup (100g) of the hickory nuts, then add the lemon zest. Add the cooked mush and rub this into the dry ingredients to form moist crumbs. Make a valley in the center of the crumbs and add the melted butter. Beat the egg yolks until frothy and lemon colored, then add the sour cream. Stir this into the crumb mixture. Beat the egg whites until stiff and forming peaks, and gently fold them into the batter. Pour the batter into the prepared *Schales* pan and scatter the remaining chopped nuts over the top. If you prefer a sweet topping, add 2 tablespoons (30g) of sugar to the nuts. Bake in the preheated oven for 25 to 30 minutes or until fully risen and set in the center. Cool on a rack. Serve at room temperature.

Watch Point: Commercial cornmeal and old-style mill-ground cornmeal vary greatly in their cooking times and textures. The cornmeal should be pre-cooked according to proportions given on the package by pouring scalding milk over it, then simmering this over a medium heat. Whisk continuously for about 15 to 20 minutes or until the cornmeal is smooth and fluffy and all the liquid has been cooked out. Set aside and cool to room temperature. Measure out 1 cup (225g) as directed.

Oatmeal Datsch
Hafermehl Datsch

This unusual Datsch has been adapted from a recipe of the late Mary Peachey, a member of the "Nebraska" Amish community in the Kishacoquillas Valley near Belleville, Pennsylvania. Mary's recipe produces a dense, rich, moist flat cake that goes well with coffee or tea.

Yield: Serves 8 to 10

Fine breadcrumbs for dusting
2 cups (250g) oat flour
1 tablespoon baking powder
1 teaspoon salt
½ cup (125g) sugar
1 cup (200g) mashed potatoes
1 cup (150g) uncooked steel-cut oatmeal
4 tablespoons (65g) melted butter
2 eggs, yolks and whites separated
1 cup (250ml) whole milk
Topping:
2 tablespoons (25g) uncooked steel-cut oatmeal
2 tablespoons (30g) coarse sugar
1 teaspoon caraway seed (or more to taste)

Preheat the oven to 375F (190C). Grease a *Schales* pan and dust this with fine breadcrumbs. Set aside.

Sift together the flour, baking powder, salt and sugar, then rub or cut in the mashed potatoes. Add the oatmeal. Make a valley in the center of the dry ingredients and add the melted butter. Beat the egg yolks until light and frothy, add the milk, then pour this into the dry ingredients and whisk until smooth. Beat the egg whites until they form stiff peaks, and fold this into the batter. Pour the batter into the prepared *Schales* pan. Make a topping by combining the oatmeal, the sugar and caraway seed; scatter this evenly over the top.

Bake in the preheated oven for 25 to 30 minutes or until fully risen and set in the center. Best when hot from the oven or reheated in a microwave oven for 1 minute on high.

Peanut Datsch
Grundniss Datsch

Jennie H. Ermentrout, or Miss Jennie to everyone who knew her, was one of the volunteer cooks during the 1920s at the Bethany Orphans' Home in Womelsdorf, Pennsylvania. Her cooking was legendary, and she contributed a number of unusual dishes like this one to the orphan home's menu in an attempt to brighten the lives of the children who lived there. Few people think of peanuts as integral to Pennsylvania Dutch cuisine, and yet they were a common feature of farmhouse gardens well into the 1940s – as many informants have reminded me. They were even the iconic feature of a now rare 1890s collectible called Peanut Spoons, an eccentric Pennsylvania Dutch Victorianism created in silver by the Keller silversmith family of Allentown.

Peanuts were mostly grown for local consumption, and *Datsch* is one way they were used. I have prepared Miss Jennie's *Datsch* with an heirloom variety of black peanut that is available from the Roughwood Seed Collection (www.RoughwoodSeeds. org). If you prefer the cake to be moister, add 1/2 cup (125ml) of sour cream to the milk. Also, as the late cookbook author Betty Herr Groff reminded me when I interviewed her several years ago, Peanut *Datsch* can be dressed up a bit by adding chocolate kisses, the same kind used for chocolate chip cookies.

Peanut Datsch

Fine breadcrumbs for dusting
2 cups (250g) all-purpose flour
2 tablespoons baking powder
1 teaspoon salt
½ cup (125g) sugar
1 cup (275g) raw, unsweetened peanut butter
½ cup (65g) chopped toasted peanuts
4 tablespoons (60ml) melted butter
2 eggs, yolks and whites separated
1 cup (250ml) whole milk or buttermilk

Topping:
4 tablespoons (25g) finely chopped toasted
   peanuts
2 tablespoons (30g) coarse sugar or crystal sugar

Preheat the oven to 375F (190C). Grease a *Schales* pan and dust with fine breadcrumbs. Set aside.

Sift together the flour, baking powder, salt and sugar. Cut in the peanut butter with a pastry cutter or work to a fine, even crumb in a food processor. Put the crumb mixture in a large work bowl. Add the chopped pea-nuts. Make a valley in the center of the crumb mixture and add the melted butter. Beat the yolks until frothy and lemon colored, then add the milk, whisk smooth and add this to the melted butter. Using a paddle or wooden spoon, stir the mixture to create sticky dough. Whisk the egg whites until stiff and forming peaks, and fold them into the batter. Pour this into the prepared *Schales* pan and pat smooth with the back of a wet spoon or paddle. Scatter the peanut and sugar mixture over the top. Using your fingers, pat or press down gently so that the top surface is smooth and the dough is evenly distributed against the edge of the pan. Bake in the preheated oven for 25 to 30 minutes or until the *Datsch* tests done in the center. Serve at room temperature.

Potato Crumb Datsch
Grumbiere Riwwel Datsch

This dense, stick-to-the-ribs old-time winter recipe traces to Flora Whitner (1861-1929), wife of Pastor Elias Helwig Whitner, whose family hailed from Numidia, in Columbia County, Pennsylvania. The only "spice" is sugar, so the cake also takes the place of dumplings when torn apart with forks while still hot. Whether hot or at room temperature, the *Datsch* was intended to be eaten with stewed apples, apple-sauce or apple butter – or even better, with very tart fruit like gooseberries or currants.

Yield: Serves 8 to 10

Fine breadcrumbs for dusting
1½ cups (375kg) all-purpose flour
¾ cup (185g) sugar
1 tablespoon baking powder
1 teaspoon salt
¾ cup (150g) mashed potatoes
4 ounces (125g) cold unsalted butter or lard
2 large eggs, yolks and whites separated
1½ cups (375ml) buttermilk

Grease a Shales pan and dust with breadcrumbs. Set aside.

Preheat the oven to 375F (190C). Sift together the flour, sugar, baking powder and salt, then rub 1 cup (100g) of the mashed potatoes into the dry ingredi-ents to form uniform loose crumbs. Put the crumbs in a food processor and add the butter chopped into small pieces. Process this until it forms crumbs. Pour the crumbs into a large work bowl and set aside 1 cup (150g) of crumbs.

Beat the egg yolks until lemon colored and frothy, then combine with the buttermilk. Add this to the crumb mixture. Beat the egg whites until stiff and forming peaks, and fold into the batter. Pour the batter into the prepared pan and spread smooth.

Take the remaining ¼ cup (50g) of mashed potatoes and work this into the reserved crumbs to make large, sticky crumbs. Scatter the crumbs over the batter and bake in the preheated oven approximately 35 to 40 minutes, or until set in the center and beginning to brown on top.

Raisin Datsch (Bethlehem Cake)

Roseine Datsch

Our recipe has been adapted from an heirloom recipe belonging to Elizabeth C. Rahn (1849-1912), a member of the Old Goshenhoppen Lutheran church in Montgomery County, Pennsylvania. Elizabeth called it Bethlehem Cake and made it rather large in size, about 16 inches (40cm) in diameter. We have cut the recipe in half so that it follows the same format as the other *Datsch* recipes in this chapter. While it is normal in the Dutch Country to think of raisin cakes or pies as specialties for old-time funerals, this particular refreshment was served during Christmas open-house entertaining in Bethlehem and Nazareth, where people flocked from house to house to see the famous Moravian *Putz* (manger scenes). Children visiting the *Putz* were also given strings of fish cookies, five to a loop, an old custom dating to the eighteenth century.

Yield: Serves 8 to 10

Fine breadcrumbs for dusting
2 cups (250g) all-purpose flour
1 tablespoon baking powder
1 teaspoon salt
½ cup (125g) light brown sugar
2 teaspoons ground cinnamon
2 teaspoons ground ginger
1 cup (200g) mashed potatoes
1 cup (125g) chopped raisins or whole Zante
    currants
½ cup (75g) coarsely chopped slivered almonds
2 teaspoons potato starch
4 tablespoon (65ml) melted butter
¼ cup (65ml) dark rum
2 eggs, yolks and whites separated
1 cup (250ml) buttermilk

Topping:
Sliced almonds

Grease a *Schales* pan and dust it with breadcrumbs. Set aside.

Preheat the oven to 375F (190C). In a large work bowl, sift together the flour, baking powder, salt, sugar, cinnamon and ginger. Add the mashed potatoes and rub this to a fine crumb. Combine the raisins and almonds and dust with the potato starch. Add this to the flour mixture.

Make a valley in the center of the flour mixture and add the melted butter and rum. Stir to make a thin batter in the center. Beat the egg yolks until lemon colored and frothy, and combine with the buttermilk. Add this to the flour mixture and work into a stiff batter. Beat the egg whites until stiff and forming peaks, then fold them into the batter. Pour the batter into the prepared pan and spread it evenly so that it touches all sides. Scatter sliced almonds over the top and bake in the preheated oven for 30 to 35 minutes or until full risen in the center. Mist with dark rum when the *Datsch* comes from the oven. Set aside on a rack to cool. Serve at room temperature or wrap in cheesecloth dipped in dark rum and store in a tight container in a cool place for 2 weeks before serving.

St. Gertrude's Day Datsch

Trudisdaag Datsch

St. Gertrude's Day (March 17) was an unofficial day of celebration in the Dutch Country, because this day marked the beginning of the planting season, especially spring grains, potatoes, cabbage and onions. An old folk saying explained it like this:

Es fiert die Trudel die Kuh zum Graut,
die Biene zum Flug
un die Ferd zum Zug.

St. Gertrude leads cows to green fodder,
sends bees into spring flight,
and draught horses to their yokes.

It was also on this day that bears were said to awaken from their winter slumbers and walk about on two feet like humans. There is no doubt that St. Gertrude of Nivelles played an important role in the folk culture of the Pennsylvania Dutch, because throughout the German Rhineland – the Old World homeland of many Pennsylvania Dutch ancestors – she was venerated since the early Middle Ages as the patron saint of cats and kitchen gardens.

Even after many Rhineland Germans converted to Protestantism during the 1500s, they continued to recognize the beneficial influence of this ancient folk saint. Just as *der Mordi* (St. Martin) retained his age-old position on the fall calendar in connection with harvesting and butchering, so too did *die Trudel* keep watch over spring planting. Unfortunately for the Dutch, Irish immigrants brought St. Patrick to America in the nineteenth century, and he has more or less preempted our old traditional observance.

St. Gertrude's *Datsch* is also the most archaic version of the traditional *Datsch* recipes in this collection, yet so wonderfully down to earth and flavorful that we decided it needed reinvention, or at least a new translation from hearth-style to modern kitchen. According to Ida Fry (1865-1960), from whom folklorist Alfred L. Shoemaker collected the recipe in 1955, this *Datsch* was originally baked in a spider, a three-legged iron skillet with a heavy, tight-fitting lid. Hot ashes went on top of the lid and underneath the pan, and it took a certain amount of cooking savvy to know just when the *Datsch* was finished. I have adjusted this baking technique to a cast-iron skillet, and the results are pretty much the same. Also, keep in mind that St. Gertrude's day occurs during Lent, so the ingredients in her *Datsch* not only reflect the old rules of Lenten fasting (no dairy, no eggs), they also anticipate what is about to be planted: spring grains, potatoes, onions and various garden herbs.

If you really want to get into the spirit of St. Gertrude's Day and observe this old-time folk tradition, then do not forget her connection to cats: a large batch of gingerbread cats will make your children happy – especially when used as rewards after undertaking a little spring cleanup in the garden. And to carry through on the theme of spring fertility (which is the underlying motif behind St. Gertrude), take small pieces of her bread and scatter them in the four corners of the garden (or a field waiting to be planted), this to please *die Gleene Leit* (the wee folk), the friendly fairies who live there, since they were thought to protect the garden from pestilence and disaster. Their "king" was the Waldmops, whom you met in the Introduction and makes more appearances here and there in this book.

St. Gertrude's
Datsch

Fine breadcrumbs for dusting
¼ ounce (7g) dry active yeast
1 cup (250ml) lukewarm potato water (98F/37C)
2 cups (250g) sifted barley flour
1 cup (125g) sifted bread flour
1 teaspoon salt
2 tablespoons ground coriander
1 tablespoon ground caraway
1 cup (200g) mashed potatoes
1 cup (125g) chopped spring onions or chives
1 tablespoon poppy seeds
2 teaspoons whole fennel seed
2 teaspoons whole flax seed
¼ cup (65ml) honey

Proof the yeast in lukewarm water sweetened with a little sugar. While the yeast is proofing, sift together 1 cup (125g) of barley flour, the bread flour, salt, ground coriander and caraway. Work in the mashed potatoes to form a fine crumb, then add the chopped onions, poppy seeds, fennel and flax.

Once the yeast is proofed and foaming vigorously, add the honey and whisk until the honey is dissolved. Make a valley in the center of the dry ingredients and add the yeast mixture. Stir to make a sticky batter, then cover and allow this to double in bulk in a warm place.

Preheat the oven to 375F (190C). Grease a 10½-inch (ca. 26cm) iron skillet or frying pan and dust with breadcrumbs or cornmeal. Once the *Datsch* has doubled in bulk, knock down and knead in the remaining 1 cup (125g) of barley flour or enough so that the dough no longer adheres to the fingers. Put this in the skillet and spread out so that it completely fills the bottom. Cover and set aside to recover. Once the dough has risen (allow about 20 to 30 minutes), remove the cover and bake in the preheated oven for 25 minutes or until the *Datsch* taps hollow in the center. Remove from the skillet and cool on a rack. Do not slice while hot; serve at room temperature.

Observation: When baking down hearth, as depicted on page 160, place a small bunch of spring onions on top of the dough before covering with the lid. The steam from the onions will create a delicious onion-flavored glaze on the top surface of the Datsch. This can be replicated in an oven if the skillet in which the *Datsch* is baked is covered with a heavy iron lid.

St. Gertrude's *Datsch* is mentioned in the Pennsylvania Dutch folk saying below, as dictated from memory many years ago by Amanda Baer Stoudt (1867-1942), grandmother of Pennsylvania Dutch folklorist John Joseph Stoudt (1912-1981).

Ebbes Griene, Ebbes Schwaatze
Ebbes Weisse fer ihre Katze.
Backt man Datsch am Trudisdaag
Streu die Grimmle wo sie mag,
Fun Eck zu Eck am Gorderand,
So wachse Dei Kreider uff das Land.

A little something green, a little
*   something black,*
A little something white for
*   her cat.*
Bake a Datsch on
*   St. Gertrude's Day*
Scatter the crumbs
*   where she directs,*
From corner to corner
*   along the garden's edge*
So that your plants will
*   thrive upon the land.*

Maple Sugar Shoofly Pie

FIVE

PIES AND TARTS

Boije un Kuche

The Pennsylvania Dutch Country has been called America's Pie Belt, and with good reason: just about everything from forest, field and garden goes into our pies. In some households, you will be served pie three times a day – without repeating the same fillings. That said, the Dutch have taken pie culture to such new levels that common terminologies do not always adequately describe our abundance of regional culinary creations – Fish Pie (no fish) and Funny Cake (a pie, not a cake) among them. Regardless, most farmhouse Dutch prefer basic hand-held pies, because they can dispense with culinary utensils and dip the pastry into breakfast coffee. Let us list a few examples from this chapter: Buttermilk Crumb Pie, Half-Moon Pie, Hard Tack Pie, Maple Sugar Shoofly Pie, Poppy Seed Tart, Railroad Pie and Slop Tarts. Rich, dark coffee from

Fair Trade plantations are a must, or go for piping hot chocolate brewed with coffee; the mocha trip is thoroughly Dutch, as you will soon discover when you try Chocolate Gribble in the pudding chapter.

During the nineteenth century, the Dutch created a wide range of specialized pie tools, like the latticework pie crust mold shown on the next page and the strip pie roller on page 166. But they also borrowed and reinvented many pies from mainstream American culture. Not surprisingly, the largest and most common category are Anglo-American pies with or without top crusts – even the term *Boi* is a Dutchification of the word pie. This would include the typical short-crusted pies with various fillings, as well as strip pies with cookie-like crusts and ornamental toppings – although these latter pies may represent a special Dutch take on

Molds for Top Pie Crusts

Harbaugh did not say much about pies, other than their homey role in rural life. Yet his collection of poems launched a revolution in Pennsylvania Dutch culture that made the "old folks" proud to share the traditions they had preserved.

Among those old-time culinary traditions were flat cakes *(Kuche)*, which I have chosen to call tarts, since that is how they are commonly translated from German into French. *Kuche* is the classic old-fashioned Pennsylvania Dutch "pie," a true pizza introduced long before Americans developed their love affair with the Italian counterpart defined largely by tomato puree (a nineteenth century invention). However, with Italian pizza now occupying such a central place in mainstream American culture, perhaps the Dutch *Kuche* will someday achieve its own niche with wild-harvest chicken-of-the-woods, chinquapins or whatever tasteful local ingredient we have at hand. The Beer Cheese Pie with Pretzel Crust (page 115) should dispel the idea that creative pizza belongs to Italy alone.

Our traditional *Kuche* are large, flat "pies" meant to feed many mouths at once; and yes, they were originally something quite similar to a pizza, with bread dough or sweetened enriched yeast-raised dough serving as a base. This dough was then covered with a myriad of toppings. Flat cakes were normally made once a week and were often large – as wide as 16 inches (45cm) in diameter, a convenient size to feed the entire farmhouse table.

Many families with large staffs of live-in help used spacious dripping pans as baking utensils, which would account for their occasional mention in old

the more ubiquitous American pie tradition. Many of these unique regionalisms appear in a rare and long-forgotten collection of heirloom recipes called *Book of Recipes for Cakes, Custards, Pies, Jellies*, printed at Gettysburg in 1869. It was compiled by a member of the Aughinbaugh family who managed to survive the horrors of the Battle of Gettysburg.

This written-from-the-heart cookbook was timely in its inclusion of Pennsylvania Dutch recipes associated with well-known period politicians, like the popular Abolitionist governors Bigler and Ritner, yet it did not fully address the pressing question of "Dutchness," which became an important cultural theme for the Pennsylvania Dutch following the Civil War – as expressed in the nostalgic dialect poems of Reverend Henry Harbaugh, also published at Gettysburg that same year under the title *Harbaugh's Harfe* (Harbaugh's Harp). Harbaugh's poems were designed to inspire the Dutch to embrace a new cultural identity imbued with a touch of patriotism; all the same, Reverend

recipes. Such large pies were a common feature in my own family's farmhouse cookery until Pennsylvania Dutch women began giving up their roomy outdoor bake ovens in favor of newfangled cook stoves – a shift that accelerated following the Civil War and the downsizing of Victorian baking expectations to accommodate the cramped space of the old time "iron dragons." After that, traditional tarts were often viewed as poverty food or simply too rustic to serve to guests, so their popularity eventually gave way to sponge cakes and other Victorian novelties, like Mary Winebrenner's 1840s Leopard Cake already mentioned in Chapter 2. Happily, I have found several treasures worth reviving and hope that you will share my enthusiasm for the real thing.

One shared feature of the Pennsylvania Dutch pie tradition was crumb toppings, whether old-style or new. Crumb toppings are called *Streussel* in German and *Riwwle* in Pennsylvania Dutch. Riwwle derives from the Pennsylfaanisch verb *riwwe* (to rub), because the crumbs were made by rubbing the ingredients together. *Riwwle* is often written in local English as rivvels, and the dried ones are sold in packages under that name. However, there seems to be some confusion in certain corners of the Dutch Country in the off-hand assertion that crumb cakes and pies were unknown in nineteenth century Pennsylvania – that this "innovation" is something purely from the 1920s onward; perhaps true of rural families too poor to afford butter or even fresh eggs, but totally in order for well-off townies.

For one thing, crumb toppings can be traced in German cookery well into the 1500s, and they were basic to the indigenous cookery in the cultural regions from which the Pennsylvania Dutch origi-nated – not to mention that there are several recipes for crumb toppings in the 1835 Silesian cookbook I consulted for the Saffron Bread recipe on page 24. Furthermore, an expansive article in German describing various types of crumb toppings appeared in the November 1877 issue of *The Confectioners Journal*, and I could cite numerous other professional American sources to put this myth to rest. The critical ethnographic question is: who made crumb toppings? Some families did and some didn't. One of the earliest crumb topping recipes in our cookbook is the Potato Crumb Datsch of Flora Whitner (page 100). Since her husband was a well-known German Reformed minister, her recipe was widely circulated among fundraising organizations in that church.

Like crumb toppings, sponge pies were easy to make and thus common throughout the nineteenth century; for this reason I was not surprised to find a recipe for gooseberry sponge pie in the 1862 edition of *Der Alte Germantown Calender*. But again, this was not fare for the poor rural Dutch, so the whole issue of who consumed crumb cakes and sponge pies really hinged on economics: which townies could afford them and which could not. Or who among the plain sects, for religious reasons, openly abjured that sort of "fancy" cuisine altogether – or quite simply did not know about it.

And finally, since you can't make a good pie without a good crust, our first handful of recipes consists of fail-safe crusts. You can use them for any of the pie recipes in this book.

Almond Pastry Dough
Mandeldeeg

This recipe came to light during the 1980s in a manuscript cookbook compiled by Catharina Bittenbender (1748-1806) of Easton, Pennsylvania. At that time, the original cookbook was still in the possession of one of her descendants, from whom I obtained the recipe. I used Catharina's pastry recipe quite effectively in 1987 while cooking a 1780s-style dinner in a swank apartment on Fifth Avenue in New York. It was amazing to see what results could be accomplished with this homey Northampton County pâté frisée taken into another world, but work it does for half-moon pies, baked dumplings, small tarts and, of course, for strip pies. The flavor is excellent and will hold its own against fruit like raspberries or even rhubarb and Seville orange. It is a perfect match for peaches or apricots. See the Raspberry Pockets on this page and the next.

Yield: Approximately 18-24

5 cups (725g) pastry flour
1 cup (250g) superfine sugar (also called caster sugar)
½ cup (65g) finely ground almonds (almond flour)
1 tablespoon (15g) salt
12 ounces (375g) unsalted butter
Yolks of 2 large eggs
6 to 9 tablespoons (90ml to 135ml) dry white wine

Sift the flour, sugar, ground almonds and salt together twice. Rub or process the butter into the dry ingredients to form crumbs. Beat the yolks until lemon colored and add 6 tablespoons (90ml) of wine. Combine with the crumbs and work into dough, adding more wine if necessary. Let the dough proof in the refrigerator at least 2 hours.

Roll out between two sheets of waxed paper, keeping the dough cold or it will become sticky. As bottom crust for large pies and strip pies, 350F (180C) is best, or it will burn easily. For small fruit tarts and half-moon pies, bake at 375F (190C) for 10 to 15 minutes or 350F (180C) for 16 to 20 minutes.

Raspberry Pockets
Himbeerdasche

The versatility of this pastry recipe can be put to the test with this easy-to-make finger food. The combination of raspberries and rosewater is an old taste preference in Pennsylvania Dutch cookery tracing at least to the eighteenth-century. Another one is the combination of pears and persimmons, which also makes an excellent filling for this pastry.

Yield: Approximately 3 dozen

1 cup (165g) fresh red raspberries
2 tablespoons (30g) sugar
1 tablespoon (30ml) rosewater or to taste
1 batch almond pastry dough
2 egg whites, lightly beaten
Crystal sugar (coarse sugar)

Preheat the oven to 350F (180C). Combine the raspberries and sugar, gently mashing the fruit as you mix, then add the rosewater. Roll out the pastry dough; using a 3-inch (7.5cm) cookie cutter with a scalloped edge, cut out rounds of dough. Put a teaspoon of the mashed berries in the center of each round. Fold over, press closed and brush the top with egg whites. Lay the pockets on an ungreased baking sheet and scatter liberally with crystal sugar. Bake in the preheated oven for 15 minutes. Cool on racks.

Basic Pie Crust (Pâté frisée)
Marrebdeeg

This is the pie crust that I developed at Roughwood for my own pies. It sculpts easily and can be cut into ornamental figures.

Yield: 1 batch (550g), sufficient for two 9-inch (23cm) pies

2 ⅓ cups (295g) all-purpose flour
8 tablespoons (125g) cold, unsalted butter
3 tablespoons (45ml) olive oil
1 egg yolk
5 tablespoons (75ml) dry white wine

Using a food processor, work the flour and butter into a fine crumb and pour this into a large work bowl. Make a valley in the center of the crumbs. In a small work bowl, beat the oil, egg and wine until thoroughly combined. Pour this into the valley and, using a fork, stir so the ingredients are fully blended into large crumbs. If the crumbs seem too dry, moisten with additional wine. Spread the crumbs on a large sheet of wax paper or baking parchment, cover with another sheet of paper. Take a rolling pin and roll the crumbs together to form dough. Turn this out into your baking pan and crimp the edges. Bake as directed in any of the pie recipes that follow.

Yeast-Raised Tart Dough
Hefe-Deeg fer Blechkuche

This versatile dough recipe has been included for use with the Cottage Cheese Tart (page 120), the Poppy Seed Tart (page 138) and Half-Moon Pies (page 128). It can also be used with Slop Tarts (page 144) and many other pies in this chapter. This is the basic "pizza" dough of Pennsylvania Dutch cookery.

Yield: Sufficient bottom crust for one 12-inch (30cm) pie

2 teaspoons (15g) dry active yeast
½ cup (125ml) warm whole milk
2 tablespoons (30g) sugar
2 cups (250g) organic bread flour
½ teaspoon salt
2 tablespoons (30ml) melted unsalted butter
1 egg
Grated zest of lemon (optional)

Proof the yeast in the milk and sugar. Sift the flour and salt into a deep work bowl and make a valley in the center. Add the yeast mixture and cover. Let the yeast proof in the flour until foaming actively, then stir down, add the butter and the well-beaten egg. Grated lemon zest can be added if you choose.

Work the ingredients together to form pliant dough and knead vigorously for about 5 minutes. Cover and let rise in a warm place until double in bulk. Knock down and roll out as thin as possible. Grease a 12-inch (30cm) baking pan and line it with the dough. Crimp or decorate the edges, cover and allow the dough to recover for 20 to 25 minutes. When ready to bake, cover the surface with filling as directed and bake in a preheated oven according to recipe instructions.

If using this as a crust with a simple crumb topping (as for example the potato crumb topping in the Datsch recipe on page 100), then bake for about 20 minutes at 400F (200C).

Apple Butter Pie
Lattwarrick Boi

Apple butter is a standard fixture of the Pennsylvania
Dutch table, used in a wide variety of ways, including
pies. This old-time coffee or breakfast cake baked
in a pie crust tastes a lot like gingerbread. It has
been adapted from the recipe of Mrs. Leo Braucher
of Shamokin, Pennsylvania; for a more interesting
texture, you can line the bottom of the pie shell with
a few thinly sliced tart apples. Or, for an entirely
old-time culinary experience, use this filling as a
spread over yeast-raised tart dough (recipe opposite).

Yield: Serves 8 to 10

1 9-inch (23cm) prepared pie shell (recipe for
  pâté frisée, opposite page)
8 tablespoons (125g) unsalted butter, room
  temperature
1 cup (250g) sugar, preferably superfine (also called
  caster sugar)
2 large eggs
½ cup (125ml) buttermilk or yoghurt
1 cup (250ml) apple butter
2 cups (250g) cake flour
1 tablespoon baking powder
1 teaspoon ground cinnamon
½ teaspoon ground cloves
1 tablespoon finely shredded orange zest
1 teaspoon anise

Preheat the oven to 375 F (190C). Cream the butter
and sugar until fluffy. Beat the eggs until lemon colored, and fold into the butter mixture. Add the sour
milk and apple butter. Sift together the flour, baking
soda and spices twice, then sift and fold this into the
batter. Scatter 1 teaspoon anise over the bottom, add
the batter and bake in the preheated oven for 35 to 40
minutes or until fully risen and set in the center.

Apple Schnitz Pie with Sweet Potatoes

Apple Schnitz Pie with Sweet Potatoes
Ebbelschnitz Boi mit Siesser Grumbiere

In this traditional-style recipe from Littlestown, Adams County, it is sweet potatoes that provide the sugar; the balance with the Schnitz is quite nice, not overly cloying as is the case with many syrupy schnitz pies. The originator of this recipe, Bertie Missouri Miller (1883-1964), was well known in the Littlestown area for her collection of heirloom sweet potatoes, and many people today still grow her Old Time White and Old Time Pink, two varieties unique to the Dutch Country.

Yield: serves 8 to 10

One 9-inch (23cm) pie shell, no top crust (recipe for pâté frisée, page 112)
2 cups (100g) tart apple schnitz (without skins)
8 ounces (250g) white or yellow sweet potatoes
4 ounces (125g) cheddar cheese shredded on the large holes of a vegetable grater
¼ teaspoon caraway seeds
1 teaspoon grated nutmeg
1 teaspoon salt
3 eggs
½ cup (50g) chopped walnuts or hickory nuts
1 tablespoon (15g) unsalted butter
Caraway seeds for garnish (optional)

Chop the schnitz in half and put them in a deep work bowl. Pour 1½ cups (375ml) boiling water over them. Cover tightly and let the schnitz infuse for an hour or two until soft and most of the liquid is absorbed. Put the schnitz in a stewing pan and add ½ cup (125ml) boiling water. Cover and simmer gently for 20 to 25 minutes or until soft and most of the liquid is cooked out. Pour this into a clean work bowl.

Pare the sweet potatoes and put them in a bowl of water with the juice of half a lemon to keep them from discoloring. When you are ready to make the pie, shred the sweet potatoes on the large holes of a vegetable grater. Combine the sweet potatoes and cooked schnitz while the schnitz are still hot. Cool for 10 minutes, then add the cheese, nutmeg, caraway and salt. Beat the eggs until frothy and lemon colored, and fold them into the sweet potato mixture. Scatter the walnuts over the bottom of the prepared pie shell, then pour the sweet potato mixture over this. Pat the batter smooth with a wooden spoon or paddle. Cut the butter into approximately 18 small bits and scatter them evenly over the top of the pie. Add a few caraway seeds as garnish or decorate with figures cut out of pie crust.

Bake in an oven preheated to 375F (190C) for 35 to 40 minutes or until set in the center. Best when served at room temperature.

Beer Cheese Pie with Pretzel Crust
Bierkees Boi mit Bretzel-Gruscht

The Pennsylvania Dutch eat salt pretzels with vanilla ice cream, so it follows that pretzels are also enjoyed with other sweet foods, including pies with fruit in them. To say the least, there are myriad variations of this classic heirloom recipe, one school delightfully savory, the other situated somewhere between second helpings and dessert. Beer cheese pie is a little-known Pennsylvania Dutch creation that gained considerable popularity in the Dutch Country during the 1920s and 1930s. Johnny Ott, chef-proprietor of the Deitsch Eck, in Lenhartsville, Pennsylvania, sold several variations of beer cheese pie, because he also sold beer cheese, a spread combining cheese, beer and finely minced chow-chow or even chopped pickled pears.

Our recipe, however, calls for fresh pears; in this case, Seckel pears, one of the oldest and most flavorful of all Pennsylvania Dutch heirloom pear varieties. Lorenz Seckel, from whom the fruit takes its name, was an eighteenth-century Pennsylvania

Dutch wine merchant who discovered this rare pear growing on his farm near what is now the Philadelphia International Airport (he was also the grandfather of Catherine Muhlenberg, mentioned in the recipe on page 48). However, if Seckel pears are not available, any pears will do, but the fruit must be firm and be best when underripe. The firm texture of underripe pears is as important as the flavor contrast with the cheese. Slicing the pears allows you to get more into the pie, if fruitiness is your thing. Some cooks omit the fruit altogether and just bake it with the beer-cheese topping.

Yield: 8 to 9 servings

1 batch pretzel crust (see recipe on page 118)
1½ pounds (750g) small, underripe Seckel pears (about 10 pears, depending on size)
2 large eggs
¼ cup (65ml) sour cream
¼ cup (65ml) light lager or ale
¼ cup (65g) light brown sugar
2 tablespoons (15g) potato starch
¼ cup (35g) grated Parmesan or Peccorino Romano cheese
½ cup (45g) sharp cheddar cheese shredded on the large holes of a vegetable grater
1 tablespoon (15g) cold unsalted butter, chopped
Grated bitter chocolate (optional)
Pretzel salt

Preheat the oven to 425F (220C). Line a shallow, well greased 11 to 12-inch (28 to 30cm) tart pan or pizza tin with the pretzel crust, making certain to make a raised border about 1 inch (2.5cm) high. Prick the bottom with a fork. Cut the pears in half lengthwise and remove the cores. Do not remove the skins. Arrange them in a circular pattern slice side down on the prepared crust, stem ends facing inwards. Or, slice the pears and arrange in a spiral pattern.

Beat the eggs until frothy and lemon colored, then add the sour cream, beer, sugar, potato starch and Parmesan cheese. Once the ingredients are thoroughly combined, pour this around and over the fruit. Scatter half of the shredded cheddar over the pears, and dot the fruit with the chopped butter. Bake in the preheated oven for 10 minutes, then reduce the heat to 375F (190C) and continue baking for 30 to 35 minutes or until the pie is set in the center and turning golden brown. Cool on a rack. Once the pie has cooled to room temperature, scatter the remaining cheese over the top. If you like, dust the pie with grated bitter chocolate or scatter a pinch of pretzel salt right before serving with glasses of chilled lager or ale.

*Beer Cheese Pie
with Pretzel Crust*

Pretzel Crust
Bretzel-Gruscht

Our favorite pretzels for this recipe are Ruth Weaver's sourdough pretzels made near Fleetwood, Pennsylvania. They are sold under the label "Ruthie's Pretzels," and not only are they extremely light and airy, they lack the unpleasant alkaline taste of lye-treated pretzels. For ordering information, refer to page 174.

Yield: one 10-inch (25cm) bottom crust

1 cup (125g) all-purpose flour
1 cup (155g) meal of unsalted pretzels (see note)
1½ teaspoons baking powder
1½ teaspoons salt
¼ cup (65ml) vegetable oil or melted unsalted butter or lard
¾ cup (190ml) cold beer, more or less

Sift together the flour, pretzel meal, baking powder and salt. Put this in a deep work bowl and make a valley in the center. Add the oil or lard, and using a wooden or horn fork, stir into the dry ingredients to form a smooth, even crumb. Add the beer 2 tablespoons (30ml) at a time, stirring until soft, pliant dough is formed. Roll this into a ball and set aside.

Grease a clean 10-inch (25cm) skillet or cake tin. Roll out the dough on a clean work surface, then transfer it to the baking utensil. Press the dough up the sides so that it reaches at least 1 inch (2.5cm) in height. Trim or crimp as desired. Bake as directed in the Beer Cheese Pie recipe (page 116) or freeze for later use.

Note: To make pretzel meal the same consistency as cornmeal, crush the pretzels in a mortar, then sift the crumbs through a coarse sieve. Continue this process until you have created 1 cup (155g). Use unsalted or low-salt pretzels.

Buttermilk Crumb Pie
Buddermillich Riwwel Boi

This old-time classic has been faithfully preserved by descendants of Mary Christine (1858-1934) of Elysburg, Pennsylvania. An accomplished cook and the wife of a well-known minister, Mrs. Christine was often called upon to entertain; thus this easy-to-make pie became one of her handy stand-ins for after-church guests and local fundraisers. The original pie was not round; rather, the filling was baked in square tin pans lined with dough, similar to the pans shown in the picture. These square pies could be sliced into small portions, each one dabbed with a little whipped cream and served with a cup of coffee.

Yield: One 9-inch (23cm) pie

1 cup (125g) all-purpose flour
2 teaspoons baking powder
¾ cup (125g) light brown sugar
½ teaspoon salt
1 teaspoon ground cinnamon
1 teaspoon freshly grated nutmeg
4 tablespoons (60g) cold unsalted butter or 2 tablespoons (30g) butter and 2 tablespoons (30g) lard
½ cup (50g) coarsely chopped walnuts
2 eggs, yolks and whites, separated
½ cup (125ml) buttermilk

Preheat the oven to 350F (180C). Sift together the flour, baking powder, sugar, salt, cinnamon and nutmeg. Add the butter and work this into crumbs. Reserve ½ cup (65g) of the crumb mixture and combine this with the chopped walnuts. Set aside.

In a separate work bowl, beat the egg yolks until lemon colored and frothy. Add the buttermilk. Whisk thoroughly and add this to the crumb mixture. Beat the whites until stiff and forming peaks, then fold this into the batter. Pour this into a prepared pie shell.

Sprinkle the reserved crumb and walnut mixture over the top and bake in the preheated oven for 45 minutes or until fully risen and set in the center. Cool on a rack, serve at room temperature.

Observation: Crumbs made by hand are far superior to those made in a food processor. Handmade crumbs are larger, coarser and thus looser; this creates a lighter and more cake-like texture. The traditional technique was to cut the crumbs together with two table knives or a horn fork. Warm fingers soften the crumbs too much.

Cottage Cheese Tart
Schmierkees Kuche

Back in 1952, a package of rare old-time Pennsylvania Dutch recipes was sent to the *Pennsylvania Dutchman* for publication, but for some reason the recipes never made it in. They had been submitted by Mark Ibach of Shiremanstown, in Cumberland County, shortly before his death and represented a massive collection gathered together by his wife, Gertrude Raffensburger Ibach (1878-1950), and her mother. The recipes included such unusual items as "Schmeltzer Noodles" (noodles with drawn butter sauce), Butterfly Cookies, and this traditional cottage cheese tart flavored with rosewater.

The rosewater caught my attention because it was a popular addition to Christmas desserts in York County and other localities west of the Susquehanna. Furthermore, decorating the tart with rosehip jam calls to mind the creative twists that made Catherine Plagemann's York County confectionery so widely admired during the 1930s and 1940s. While Plagemann's *Fine Preserving* was eventually republished by M.F.K. Fisher, it does not contain recipes for tarts, so I consulted Emmy Braun's *Neues Kochbuch* (New Cookbook), one of the great classics of Palatine cookery, since it features a few traditional rosehip recipes. The Pennsylvania Dutch, like their Palatine cousins, considered rosehips essential to their cookery, more or less taking up the role of pomegranates. In short, the rosehip became the symbolic pomegranate in Pennsylvania Dutch folk art and even assumed a position of respect in traditional powwow medicine.

Yield: Serves 16 to 20

1 batch yeast-raised tart dough (page 112)
1 cup (225g) cottage cheese
6 tablespoons (90ml) cream
2 tablespoons (30ml) melted unsalted butter
½ teaspoon salt
½ cup (125g) sugar
2 tablespoons (15g) potato starch or flour
2 large eggs, separated
Grated zest of ½ lemon
¼ cup (65ml) rosewater
½ cup (50g) coarsely shredded sharp cheese
  (such as cheddar)
Rosehip jam (see sidebar)

Preheat the oven to 325F (165C). Put the cottage cheese, cream, melted butter, salt, sugar, potato starch and egg yolks in a food processor or Vitamix. Process the ingredients until thick and creamy (about

3 minutes), then pour into a deep work bowl. Add the grated lemon zest and rosewater. Beat the egg whites until stiff and forming peaks, and fold them into the cottage cheese mixture. Pour this into a prepared 12-inch (30cm) pie shell of yeast-raised tart dough and scatter shredded cheese over the top. Bake the pie in the preheated oven for 45 to 50 minutes or until the filling has risen up and begun to turn golden brown. Remove from the oven and cool on a rack. Once cool, ornament with rosehip jam.

Observation: For greater eye appeal, you can brush the crust with a mixture of egg yolk and cream right before putting it into the oven. This will give the crust a golden brown hue.

Rosehip Jam
Lattwarrick fun Hagebutte

This recipe produces a richly colored thick jam fragrant of rosehips; the secret is to add rose-water at the last minute. Cooked rosehip puree is naturally deep orange and should retain that color, although prolonged cooking will darken it. To prepare the rosehips, nip off the buds and stems and cover with water in a large stewing pan. Bring to a hard boil, then reduce the heat and simmer 40 minutes or until fruit is soft. Cover and stand overnight in the refrigerator so that the hips become a thick mass with most of the liquid absorbed. Press through a fine strainer and reserve the puree. Since different types of rosehips yield different quantities of paste, it is not possible to provide exact measurements. However, you should begin with at least 10 pounds (5kg) of rosehips in order to make enough paste for jam. Then follow the instructions below.

Yield: 6 cups (1.5 liters) of jam

1½ cups (375ml) rosehip puree
1½ cups (375ml) sweet white Zinfandel or
  a similar wine
1½ teaspoons grated zest of lemon
¼ cup (65ml) lemon juice

1 package Sure-Jell
½ cup (125ml) rosewater
4½ cups (1.25 kg) sugar
6 teaspoons (30ml) rosewater

Put the puree, wine, lemon zest, lemon juice and Sure-Jell in a large preserving pan. Bring this to a rolling boil. Add the ½ cup (125ml) of rose-water, stir, then add the sugar. Bring to a full boil and boil 1 minute. Skim off scum and pour into hot sani-tized jelly jars. Add 1 teaspoon of rosewater to each jar. Seal and turn the jars upside down for 5 minutes. After 5 minutes set them upright and store in a cool dark place. The jam will set in about 1 hour after the jars are cool.

Fish Pie
Fisch Boi

First of all, fish pie is not made with fish. Where it acquired this unusual name has not yet been pinpointed, although in those areas of the Dutch Country where it is popular, all sorts of colorful theories abound. What we do know is that Fish Pie is connected in some way with the *Drierwirbel* (spinning trinity), three interlocking fish commonly depicted in folk art, especially on earthenware dishes. This image is said to represent the Christian Trinity (three fish as a triplicated symbol of Christ), but in fact, the real symbolism is rooted in pre-Christian religion and the magical power of three. The iconic fishes may allude to an ancient Celtic fish cult along the Rhine, focused on the seasonal cycles of salmon or shad. Whatever the case, these deep-rooted connections with the Old Religion were brought to America by the Pennsylvania Dutch.

Following that theme, shad would make sense in Pennsylvania Dutch terms, since fish pie was originally associated with April 1 when the ice melt began to draw these migratory fish in from the sea. Furthermore, the pie evolved along the Susquehanna River, which places its origins squarely in an area once devoted to shad fishing. This is why the pie is more or less endemic to the region of Pennsylvania northwest of Reading and centering on Sunbury, where some people claim it was invented. The oldest printed recipe found thus far appeared in a 1938 cookbook from Ravine, Pennsylvania, although field interviews have determined that the pie dates back at least to the 1890s.

Historical conjecture aside, if we were to categorize fish pie by generic type, it appears to be a sub-category of the classic Berks County strip pie: cookie-dough crust with a syrupy custard-like filling. There are also several types of fish pie; some contain eggs, some do not. Many are flavored with molasses, others with lemons or oranges. In this case, I am using the recipe of Edna I. Daniel (1901-1988) of Rebuck, Pennsylvania, in Northumberland County. She was one of the culinary mentors of Erma Lettich (1911-1998), who lived on a nearby farm in Sacramento, and who became a county-wide legend as a baker of traditional cakes and pastries.

Yield: One 8-inch (20cm) pie

Pie Filling:
½ **cup (125ml) unsulfured molasses**
½ **cup (90g) light brown sugar**
¼ **cup (65ml) fresh lemon juice**
1 cup (250ml) spring water or strong coffee
2 tablespoons (15g) potato starch or cake flour
2 tablespoons (15g) baking cocoa
1 teaspoon ground cinnamon
2 eggs, separated

Crust:
1 cup (170g) light brown sugar
4 tablespoons (65g) unsalted butter or lard
¼ **teaspoon salt**
1½ **teaspoons baking powder**
½ **cup (125ml) clabbered raw milk or buttermilk**
Approximately 2 cups (250g) all-purpose flour

To make the filling, combine all the ingredients listed above (except the eggs) in a deep saucepan. Bring to a rolling boil until it thickens and whisk smooth, then set aside to cool.

Then make the crust by creaming together the brown sugar, butter or lard, and salt. Dissolve the baking powder in the milk and add this to the crust mixture. Sift in the flour until it forms stiff dough. Chill in the refrigerator 2 hours to ripen. When ready to bake, preheat the oven to 350F (180C). Take an 8-inch (20cm) pie pan and put half the dough in it. Using your fingers, gently press down on the dough and spread it over the bottom of the pan so that it comes up the sides to the top edge. Crimp the edges.

Beat the egg yolks until frothy, then whisk them into the chilled filling mixture. Beat the egg whites until stiff and forming peaks, and fold them into the batter. Fill the prepared crust. Using your fingers, spread the remaining dough on a clean work surface, then cut it into 9-inch (23cm) strips or make ornamental figures (I have made fish). Lay these over the filling; if using strips, pinch or attach the ends to the dough in the pan. Bake in the preheated oven for approximately 30 minutes or until the crust tests done and the filling has set in the center. Cool on a rack and serve at room temperature.

Green Apple Pie
with Grapefruit and Lovage

The Dutch farmhouse kitchen wasted nothing, even the green apples that fall off the trees in the summer. Imperfect, perhaps containing a worm or two, these apples were looked upon as opportunity rather than waste. The idea of dressing them up with a touch of grapefruit and lovage is a brilliant solution.

We are not certain who in the Dutch Country was the first to try this novel combination, yet it seems to trace back to the *Nei-Deitsch* Movement in the 1920s when many regional cooks began to look for clever ways to reinvent traditional dishes. This is probably when Dutch-style duck first appeared (duck baked with green butter pears, grapefruit and lovage), and was followed by a host of other variations.

The nice thing about this pie is its adaptability. Some cooks prefer top crusts, while others like strip pie toppings due to the added sweetness – or no topping at all, leaving the custard filling to turn

golden yellow on the surface. I prefer this latter approach. Once the pie is chilled and ready to serve, dust it with finely minced fresh lovage leaves and tiny shreds of candied grapefruit rind. It is excellent when accompanied by Prosecco or Champagne.

Yield: one 10-inch pie

4 cups (400g) cored, chopped green apples, skins left on (see note)
²/₃ cup (160ml) freshly squeezed grapefruit juice
¾ cup (185g) sugar
½ teaspoon salt
1 tablespoon minced lovage
1 teaspoon grated zest of grapefruit rind
2 large eggs
¾ cup (180ml) sour cream or buttermilk
finely minced lovage and shredded candied grapefruit rind as garnish

Preheat the oven to 350F (180C). Combine the apples, grapefruit juice, sugar and salt in a stew pan, then cover and simmer the mixture over a low heat until the apples are soft (about 15 minutes).

Pour this into a food processor or blender, add the lovage and grapefruit zest, then reduce the mixture to a thick puree. Pour into a work bowl to cool. Once room temperature beat the eggs until frothy and lemon color, add the sour cream and whisk this into the fruit batter. Pour this into a prepared pie shell and bake in the preheated oven for 55 to 60 minutes or until the filling is set and golden color on top. Serve chilled with a garnish of minced lovage and shredded candied grapefruit rind.

Note: If you do not have access to green apples, Granny Smiths can be substituted. You can also make this pie with green or underripe pears. In case you cannot find lovage, you can create a similar flavor by mixing fresh parsley and celery leaves in equal proportions.

Groundcherry Strip Pie
Juddekarrsche Boi

In the Dutch Country, groundcherries peak during the hottest days of July and August and then continue until frost. There are many varieties, the New Hanover strain being the closest to tiny currant tomatoes in flavor. Like tomatoes, groundcherries are improved with a dash of nutmeg. But they also marry well with peaches, pineapples and even mangoes, so you are likely to find many intriguing pie variations at farm stands and markets throughout the summer. This recipe is a combination of several that I have tried and emphasizes the fruitiness of the groundcherries.

Yield: One 8-inch (20cm) pie

2 cups (300g) groundcherries
½ cup (100g) coarsely chopped fresh pineapple
3 tablespoons (45ml) fresh lemon juice
1 teaspoon grated orange zest
2 tablespoons potato starch
½ teaspoon freshly grated nutmeg
½ cup (90g) light brown sugar
Strip pie dough (see recipe this page)

Preheat the oven to 400F (200C). Remove the groundcherries from their husks and rinse thoroughly. Put them in a work bowl with the pineapple, lemon juice and orange zest. Sift together the potato starch, nutmeg and brown sugar, and combine this with the fruit mixture. Pour this into a prepared pie shell. Make strips of dough with the strip pie crust and lay these over the fruit, pinching the ends so that they seal with the bottom crust. Bake in the preheated oven for 10 minutes, then reduce the heat to 350F (175C) and continue baking for 35 to 40 minutes or until the center is thoroughly cooked. Cool on a rack and serve at room temperature.

Strip Pie Crust
Deeg Schtreefe fer Boije

The basic recipe for country-style strip pie dough is very simple. The recipe here is still used extensively at Berks County bake sales and can be traced to Amelia Barto Mosser (1850-1930), who was well-known in the 1920s for her lemon strip pies. Strip pie dough is only used for the strips across the top, not for the pastry shell itself. Called "sweet dough" *(siesser Deeg)* in Pennsylvania Dutch, this recipe will produce enough strips for 2 or 3 pies. Cut the recipe in half if you are using the dough only for the groundcherry pie above. Otherwise, you can freeze the extra dough for later use.

1 cup (250g) superfine sugar
8 ounces (125g) unsalted butter
1 egg
½ cup (125ml) sour cream
1½ teaspoons baking powder
2 cups (250g) pastry flour

Cream butter and sugar, then beat the egg until lemon colored and combine it with the sour cream. Add this to the butter and sugar, then sift together the baking powder and flour. Sift this into the wet ingredients and work into soft dough. Form into a ball, cover and allow the dough to mellow in the refrigerator for 2 to 3 hours. Roll out while cold and cut into narrow strips. Lay the strips in a parallel pattern on top of your pie and bake as directed in the recipe above.

Half-Moon Pies with Pumpkin Filling
Halbmond Boije mit Karrebse Fillsel

This is a recipe with a fascinating history. In 1949, Muhlenberg College professor Preston A. Barba wrote to the late folklife scholar Dr. Don Yoder lamenting the fact that the Pennsylvania Dutch cookbook he was working on with Ann Hark would not be finished in time for Christmas. Now considered a classic, the Hark and Barba cookbook was published the following year, but many recipes had to be jettisoned in order to meet the publishing deadline. Barba sent the unpublished recipes to Don Yoder's mother with the idea that she might be able to use them at the Kutztown Folk Festival, where she appeared for

many years as a demonstrator. Those recipes were lost to history until they recently came to light in Dr. Yoder's papers. So I salvaged the pumpkin filling and found that it worked very well with the almond pastry, and since it too originated from the Easton area, we now have the satisfaction of bringing two rare recipes together in what is certainly a happy marriage of history and culinary art – doubly so because I used the picturesque and richly flavorful Nanticoke pumpkins that have been grown in the region since pre-colonial times (depicted above and opposite).

1 batch Almond Pastry (page 110)
1 cup (275g) cooked pureed pumpkin
¼ cup (45g) light brown sugar
¼ cup (45g) Zante currants
¼ cup (35g) chopped hazelnuts, walnuts,
  or almonds
2 tablespoons (15g) cracker crumbs or
  bread crumbs
1 teaspoon ground coriander
¾ teaspoon ground cardamom
½ teaspoon ground mace
1 teaspoon grated zest of Seville orange or lemon
2 egg yolks
1 egg white

Prepare the pastry dough as instructed and set aside. To make the filling, steam the pumpkin until tender, and press it through a colander or chinoise. The pumpkin puree must contain as little moisture as possible. Preheat the oven to 350F (180C).

Combine the pumpkin, brown sugar, currants and nuts. Sift together the cracker crumbs and spices, then add this to the pumpkin batter. Flavor with orange zest, then beat the egg yolks until frothy and add them to the mixture. Whisk the egg white until stiff and forming peaks, and fold this into the filling. Take a cold marble or glass rolling pin (the Dutch also used locally-made slate pins) and roll out the reserved pastry dough about ¼-inch (6mm) thick on a clean work surface. Cut into 4-inch (10cm) rounds. Place a tablespoon scoop of filling in the center of each round, and fold over to form half-moon pies. Pinch the edges shut or press with a fork. Prick 3 holes in the top of each pie to create vents for steam (this will help prevent their popping open) and stick a whole blanched almond or hazelnut in the middle of the pie edge (see photo). Set the pies on ungreased baking sheets and bake in the preheated oven for 16 to 20 minutes or until pale golden. Cool on racks and serve at room temperature.

Hard Tack Pie or Poor House Pie
Kraeker Boi

I remember seeing this distinctive pie many years ago at several farmers markets in Berks County, then sometime during the late 1970s it disappeared. It was known locally as Poor House Pie, because it was served at the county poor house well into the 1930s. In spite of its name and lowbrow origin, the pie became one of those mascot dishes for the "good old days." Let us say it enjoyed a large local following, and many people still ask for it. The old-time pie was dense and dry and meant to be hand-dipped in fresh morning coffee or broken up in hot milk and eaten like gruel. From a distance it resembled a head of cauliflower baked in a pie shell, because the crumb part would rise up into a hill at the center.

As its original name would suggest, the key ingredient in the pie was hard tack, a type of crisp cracker no longer manufactured; oyster crackers can provide a reasonable substitute. Use a pastry cutter to reduce them to the consistency of steel-cut oatmeal. As luck would have it, a real piece of 1896 U.S. Army hard tack recently surfaced at auction, glued into the Spanish-American War-era scrapbook of Pennsylvania soldier Harry T. Hyndman, so we know exactly what the original hard tack looked like: a large flat rectangular water cracker with rows of holes punched into the surface. No salt, just dry as the desert.

1 prepared 9-inch (23cm) pie shell
2 cups (150g) unsalted oyster crackers crushed to oatmeal consistency
1 cup (200g) warm, freshly mashed potatoes
½ cup (65g) all-purpose flour
1 tablespoon baking powder
½ teaspoon salt
¾ cup (185g) sugar
6 tablespoons (90g) unsalted butter or lard
1 large egg, separated
½ cup (125ml) buttermilk or sour cream
1 tablespoon coarse sugar

Preheat the oven to 375F (190C). Prepare a 9-inch (23cm) pastry shell and set aside.

Put the cracker meal in a deep work bowl and add the potatoes. Using your fingers, work this into large sticky crumbs. The moisture from the potatoes should soften the cracker meal.

In a separate work bowl, sift together the flour, baking powder, salt and sugar. Then work the butter into the flour mixture to form evenly textured crumbs. Combine this with the cracker-and-potato mixture, rubbing them together so that they attain a uniform consistency. Remove 1 cup (150g) of the crumb mixture and set aside.

Beat the egg yolk until frothy, then combine with the buttermilk. Fold this into the crumbs. Then beat the egg white until it forms stiff peaks and fold this into the crumb mixture as well. At this point, the batter should resemble thick mashed potatoes. Pour it into the prepared pie shell and spread it evenly with the back of a large spoon dipped in cold water. Shape the filling so that it is higher in the middle than around the edges, then scatter the reserved crumbs over the top. Sprinkle coarse sugar over the crumbs and bake in the preheated oven for 30 to 35 minutes or until the pie turns golden brown on top and is set in the center.

Jolly Molly's Saffron Pie
Tschalli Mollis Safferich Boi

In real life, Jolly Molly was Mary Brown Hellman (1913-1991), the owner of two restaurants called Jolly Molly's that began in Newmanstown, Pennsylvania, in 1945 and then relocated to downtown Lebanon

in 1975. Her restaurant was well known regionally for high quality Pennsylvania Dutch cookery, but perhaps even more famous was the softball team she sponsored that became a sports legend and even won the nationals in 1987. The Internet is loaded with lore about the Jolly Molly Club, as the team was called, but time seems to have forgotten the original Jolly Molly, whose extraordinary culinary legacy is the reason for this recipe. A clever variation of lemon sponge pie, Jolly Molly's Saffron Pie came to us from one of the former pastry cooks for the restaurant. While the pie was only served at special events, and mostly by request, it remains an iconic tribute to the way Lebanon County still cooks with saffron.

Yield: Serves 8 to 10

2 tablespoons (30g) unsalted butter
¾ cup (185g) sugar
2 tablespoons (15g) cake flour
2 tablespoons (15g) potato starch
2 teaspoons freshly grated nutmeg
½ teaspoon ground cardamom
Grated zest of 1 lemon
¼ teaspoon ground saffron
½ cup (125ml) milk
½ cup (125ml) sour cream
3 eggs, yolks and whites separated
One 9-inch (23cm) pie shell (no top crust)

Preheat the oven to 450F (230C). In a deep work bowl, work the butter and sugar together to form fluffy, snow-like crumbs, then add the pastry flour, potato starch, nutmeg, cardamom and lemon zest. Dissolve the saffron in the milk. Beat the egg yolks until lemon colored and frothy, then add the milk and sour cream. Combine this with the sugar mixture. Beat the egg whites until they form stiff peaks, and fold them into the batter. Pour this into a prepared pie shell and bake in the preheated oven for 10 minutes. Reduce the heat to 350F (180C) and continue baking until the pie is set and has turned golden brown on the top (about 20 to 25 minutes). Once set, remove from the oven and cool on a rack. Serve slightly chilled or at room temperature.

Lemon Crumb Pie
Lemmon Riwwel Boi

This delicious heirloom recipe belonged to Edna Kline Roland (1895-1985), the wife of Akron, Pennsylvania, teacher and high school principal Loyd H. Roland. Mrs. Roland was well known in local church affairs, and her pie often appeared at community fundraisers, including benefits for the town park, now named in honor of her late husband.

Yield: two 9-inch (23cm) pies

Two 9-inch (23cm) pie shells
1¼ cup (155g) all-purpose flour
1 cup (250g) sugar
1 tablespoon baking powder
½ teaspoon salt
6 tablespoons (90g) unsalted butter
Grated zest of 1½ lemons
2 eggs, yolks and whites separated
1½ cups (375ml) buttermilk
5 tablespoons fresh lemon juice
Lemon sugar

Prepare the pie shells and set aside. Preheat the oven to 350F (175C). Sift together the flour, sugar, baking powder and salt. Rub in the butter to form loose crumbs and add the lemon zest. Make a valley in the center of the dry ingredients.

In a separate work bowl, beat the egg yolks until frothy, then add the buttermilk and lemon juice. Pour this into the valley in the dry ingredients and stir to form thick batter. Beat the egg whites until stiff and forming peaks, and fold into the batter. Divide the batter evenly between the two prepared pie shells and bake in the preheat oven for 45 minutes or until fully risen and turning golden brown on top. Scatter lemon sugar over the pies, then cool on racks. Serve at room temperature or slightly chilled.

Quite often, there were Amish people camped out in the parking lot, their buggies loaded with local produce and baked goods in an impromptu farm market. My mother always made a beeline for a certain elderly woman, a regular on the scene who baked the best lemon sponge pies going – at least I thought so; mother even managed to wheedle the recipe out of her. Thus, lemon sponge pie became my birthday "cake," and every year it would appear on March 13 as if by magic. It was also one of the first Pennsylvania Dutch recipes I learned to make myself; and now, I share it with you. When properly baked, it should develop a dark honey-brown top. The filling separates into two zones: custard on the bottom and a layer of lemon sponge on top.

Yield: One 9-inch (23cm) pie, serves 8 to 10

2 tablespoons (30g) butter
1 cup (250g) sugar
2 tablespoons (15g) pastry flour
Grated zest of 1 lemon
3 eggs, yolks and whites separated
1 cup (250ml) milk
5 tablespoons (75ml) lemon juice
1 prepared 9-inch (23cm) pie shell (no top crust)

Work the butter, sugar and flour to an even crumb consistency and add the lemon zest. Beat the egg yolks until light and frothy, then add to the butter mixture. Gradually add the lemon juice and milk to form a batter. Beat the egg whites until stiff and standing in peaks. Fold this into the batter. Pour into an 8 to 9 inch pastry shell and bake in an oven preheated to 450F (230C) for 10 minutes. Reduce the heat to 350F (180C) and continue baking 30 minutes or until the pie is set.

Lemon Sponge Pie
Lemmon Schwaam Boi

When I was a small boy, my parents moved to Upstate New York – a chapter in my life I have always referred to as my "Winter Exile." This difficult separation from the lush farmlands of Pennsylvania necessitated periodic visits to my grandmother, who lived in Chester County. The scenic drive back and forth took us along Route 15, which follows the Susquehanna River for many miles above Harrisburg. Our pit stop both ways was always the Dutch Pantry near Selinsgrove; it offered on the way down the nostalgic tastes of "home" and on the way back a last call for sweet bologna, scrapple and similar necessities for a well-stocked Pennsylvania kitchen in exile.

Mango Schnitz Pie
Mango Schnitz Boi

One of the very best gardeners I had the pleasure of employing at Roughwood during the early 1980s was a Pennsylvania Dutchman by the name of Jonas Slonaker. He was the most meticulous garden manager I have ever met and was also an accomplished cook, training he had acquired while growing up with his grandmother. Jonas used to sing hilarious bowdlerized hymns while he worked, and I have always imagined that is how he cast his magic spell over the plants. For certain, when he sang at the stove his food turned out nothing short of glorious.

Several years prior to coming to Roughwood, Jonas had considered joining the Amish sect, and that spiritual journey took him to an Amish settlement in Guatemala. It was there that he learned to cook a new sort of Pennsylvania Dutch cuisine, which fused traditional dishes with Central American ingredients. Mango Schnitz Pie was just one of several tropical Pennsylvania Dutch creations that Jonas used to share over lunch. Jonas was also one of the first people to point out to me that Pennsylvania Dutch cuisine was undergoing fascinating changes, and that these distant connections with exotic locales were yielding up unusual tastes, innovative dishes and a whole new world where tradition was assuming a totally different meaning.

Yield: Serves 8 to 10

8 ounces (250g) mango schnitz (sliced dried mangoes)
1½ cups (375ml) boiling water or mango juice
1 tablespoon (7.5g) potato starch
½ teaspoon ground cinnamon
¼ teaspoon ground allspice
½ cup (125g) sugar
2 large eggs
1 cup (250ml) thick coconut milk (consistency of yoghurt)
1½ tablespoons grated lime zest
One 9 to 10 inch (23 to25cm) prepared pie shell

Chop the mango schnitz into small, bite-size pieces and then put them in a deep work bowl. Add the boiling water or mango juice, cover and stand 30 to 40 minutes or until the mango bits are soft. Drain and return the mango to the work bowl. Combine the starch, cinnamon, allspice and sugar, and stir this into the mangos. Beat the eggs until lemon colored and frothy, then combine with the coconut milk. Add this to the mango mixture and fold in the lime zest.

Pour this into the prepared pie crust and bake in an oven pre-heated to 350F (180C) for 40 to 50 minutes or until set in the center. Serve at room temperature or slightly chilled, garnished with shreds of lime zest or a mixture of lime and orange zest.

Mango Schnitz Pie

Maple Sugar Shoofly Pie
(Ahorn Zucker Schuflei Boi)

With a texture similar to cornbread, this Somerset County breakfast pie is delicious when served warm from the oven with maple syrup drizzled over it. For a gooey wet bottom texture, spread 4 tablespoons (60ml) of maple syrup over the bottom of the pie shell before adding the batter. While adding the batter, drizzle 2 additional tablespoons (30ml) of maple syrup over the mixture. Add the crumbs as called for and bake.

Yield: Serves 8 to 10

Crumb Topping:
½ cup (65g) all-purpose flour
¼ cup (65g) organic maple sugar
2 tablespoons (30g) cold unsalted butter

Pie Filling:
1¼ cups (155g) all-purpose flour
½ cup (85g) organic maple sugar
1 tablespoon (5g) baking powder
1 teaspoon salt
4 tablespoons (65g) unsalted cold butter
1 egg, separated
½ cup (125ml) organic maple syrup
½ cup (125ml) sour cream
2 teaspoons vanilla extract

Preheat the oven to 350F (180C) and prepare the crumb topping as directed. Rub or chop together with a pastry cutter the flour, maple sugar and butter until fine crumbs are formed. Set aside.

In a large work bowl, prepare the pie filling by sifting together the flour, maple sugar, baking powder and salt. Work in the butter to form loose crumbs.

In another work bowl, beat the egg yolk until lemon colored and frothy, and whisk in the maple syrup. Combine this with the sour cream and vanilla, then add this to the crumb mixture, stirring gently to create a thick batter. Beat the egg white until it forms peaks, and fold it in to the filling. Prepare a 9-inch (23cm) pie shell and add the batter, spreading it evenly with the back of a spoon dipped in cold water. Scatter the reserved crumbs over the top, smoothing them with the back of a fork. Scatter 1 tablespoon of coarse maple sugar or vanilla sugar over the top. Bake in the preheated oven for 45 to 50 minutes or until fully risen and set in the center. Serve warm from the oven or cool on a rack and serve at room temperature.

Poppy Seed Tart
Mohnkuche

Not overly sweet, this is one of my favorite Pennsylvania Dutch recipes. Poppy seed tart was at one time a standard fixture for Harvest Home, Christmas and Easter dinners. It was even served at weddings. For a Christmas touch, add allspice and cardamom to the filling; for Easter, use instead ground star anise and scatter a tablespoon of anise seeds in the baking pans before adding the egg crusts. Even better, add the anise seeds to the crust dough.

Several years ago, I came across a traditional baking tin for poppy seed tart at a Berks County flea market; who would have guessed that it dated from the 1850s. Measuring 10 inches (25cm) at the rim, 9 inches (23cm) inside the rim, and ¾-inch (1.8 cm) high, this is a classic *Schales* pan, although not as broad as most (see photo on page 167).

Critical Watch Point: For this recipe, you will need 2 shallow tart pans no more than ¾-inch (1.8cm) deep. The deeper the baking pans, the longer the tarts will take to bake, and if the tarts remain too long in the oven, this will cause the delicate egg crust to darken and crumble. To avoid this, you may want to line the tart pans with baking parchment, since the tarts will be easier to remove and less likely to overcook on the bottom.

Yield: Two 9-inch (23cm) tarts (8 to 10 servings each)

Prepare the Crust:
1 batch Egg Crust (see sidebar for directions)

After the egg crust is prepared and cooling in the refrigerator, make the crumb topping as follows:

Crumb Topping:
1¼ cups (150g) all-purpose flour
¼ cup (45g) light brown sugar
6 tablespoons (90g) unsalted butter
2 tablespoons (15g) confectioner's (10X) sugar

Sift together the flour and brown sugar. Heat the butter in a small saucepan and melt it (do not boil or clarify). Pour hot over the flour mixture and, using a fork, stir into the flour to form crumbs. Once cool, dust with confectioner's sugar and set aside. Now prepare the tart filling.

Filling:
8 ounces (250g) poppy seeds
3 ounces (100g) light brown sugar
1 cup (250ml) strong coffee
½ cup (125ml) cream
½ teaspoon salt
¼ cup (30g) cracker dust or fine breadcrumbs
½ teaspoon ground cinnamon
2 ounces (50g) chopped hickory nuts
½ ounce (13g) grated bitter chocolate
3 egg whites

To prepare the filling, pour the poppy seeds, sugar and coffee into a broad saucepan and bring to a gentle simmer. Cover and cook for about 10 minutes or until the poppy seeds are soft and all the liquid has evaporated. Set aside and cool.

While the filling is cooling, preheat the oven to 350F (175C). Roll out the cold egg crust and line the baking tins. Then add the cream, salt, cracker dust (or fine breadcrumbs), cinnamon, bitter chocolate and chopped nuts to the filling mixture. Beat the egg whites until they form stiff peaks, and fold them into the filling. Pour this over the prepared crusts and spread in a thin, even layer. Scatter the reserved crumbs over the tops. Bake in the preheated oven for 35 to 40 minutes or until the tarts test done in the center. Cool on a rack, then scatter 1 tablespoon of vanilla sugar over each tart (optional). These tarts can be frozen for later use. They are excellent with strong coffee.

Egg Crust
Oier Deeg

This rich, flavorful crust is often pre-baked and then filled with thickened stewed fruit or other types of cooked fillings. It can also be used with fruit tarts or as strip pie crust. And not the least, it makes excellent roll-out cookies, with a texture akin to shortbread.

Yield: Sufficient for two 9-inch (23cm) tarts

3 cups (375g) pastry flour
8 ounces (250g) unsalted butter
6 hard-cooked egg yolks
¾ cup (135g) confectioner's (10-X) sugar
2 tablespoons (30g) chicken or goose fat, lard or vegetable oil
Grated zest of 1 lemon

Rub together 2½ cups (315g) of pastry flour and the butter to form fine, even crumbs. Grate the yolks as fine as possible and work them into the crumb mixture along with the confectioner's sugar, shortening and lemon zest. Gently knead the dough on a clean work surface (preferably a cold marble slab) and work the remaining ½ cup (60g) of flour into the dough until it develops a soft, spongy texture. Form into a ball and refrigerate until required. Roll out for crusts while cold. For baking directions, refer to the recipe on page 126.

Purple Pump Pie
Purpur Bump Boi

There is a real place called the Purple Pump, although it's not a town, just a crossroads near Franklin Square, Pennsylvania, where a functioning cast-iron pump has stood for over a century. It was put there originally to water horses, now it has become a local landmark when giving directions. No one is certain who decided to paint it bright purple, but it has been that way as long as anyone can remember, and from time to time it quietly receives a fresh coat of color.

Directly across the road from the pump is a tavern where farmers and hunters hang out. It was there that I first tasted this pie, because all around the Mahantongo Valley elderberries grow in glorious abundance, and at the time of my visit, a handsome harvest was sitting heaped in trays on the bar counter. With satisfied grins and purple teeth, the gentlemen gathered there were enjoying an improvised pie fest consisting of several kinds of elderberry pies. After rivers of beer and other tongue-loosening refreshments, it gradually came out that they were honoring the pump, since it and the pies shared the same color.

Yield: Serves 8 to 10

4½ cups (1 pound/500g) fresh or frozen ripe
  elderberries (see note)
½ teaspoon ground cassia
1 cup (250ml) red wine
3 large eggs, yolks and whites separated
¾ cup (80ml) sour cream
Grated zest of 1 orange
½ cup (125g) superfine sugar (also called
  caster sugar)

2 tablespoons (15g) potato starch
2 tablespoons (15g) cake flour
2 tablespoons (30g) unsalted butter
¼ cup (65ml) Sambucca
1 prepared 9-inch (23cm) pie shell (no top crust)

Preheat the oven to 450F (230C). Put the elderberries in a stewing pan with the cassia and wine. Cover tightly and cook the berries over a medium heat until they are reduced to mush (about 15 to 20 minutes). Remove and strain through a fine sieve or chinois. This should yield 1½ cups (375ml) of liquid. Pour this into a large work bowl to cool; discard the mash.

While the elderberry liquid is cooling, beat the egg yolks until lemon colored and frothy, and add the sour cream and orange zest. Sift together the sugar, potato starch and cake flour, then rub this into the butter to form soft crumbs. Add this to the egg mixture. Then add the reserved elderberry liquid and Sambucca. Beat the egg whites until stiff and forming peaks, and fold them into the batter. Pour this into the prepared pie shell. Bake in the preheated oven for 10 minutes. Reduce the heat to 350F (180C) and continue baking for 20 to 25 minutes or until set in the center. Cool on a rack. Serve slightly chilled or at room temperature. The top of the pie will turn mauve-brown; this is normal.

Note: If you do not have access to fresh or frozen elderberries, you may substitute elderberry juice concentrate, which is sold online. Extracting juice from an infusion of water and dried elderberries (also available online) will not yield the sharp fruity flavor that makes this pie so striking.

Railroad Pie or Rivvel Pie
Reggelweg Boi odder Riwwelboi

Like Railroad Cake (page 49), this too was a popular snack sold by hucksters at train stations throughout the Dutch Country. In the days before dining cars, fresh fruit, peanuts, cookies, pretzels and pies were more or less standard fare for hungry travelers who bartered for their food through open windows of the train. The pie was also popular with owners of boarding houses and cheap hotels, because it made ideal finger food, good for dipping into morning coffee.

Yield: Serves 8 to 10

1 prepared 9-inch (23cm) pie shell
1¼ cup (155g) all-purpose flour
¾ cup (185g) sugar
1 teaspoon ground cinnamon
1 tablespoon baking powder
½ teaspoon salt
4 ounces (125g) unsalted cold butter
2 large eggs
1½ cup (375ml) buttermilk

Topping:
1 tablespoon coarse sugar
1 teaspoon ground cinnamon

Preheat the oven to 350F (180C). Sift together the flour, sugar, cinnamon, baking powder and salt. Then work this to a coarse crumb with the cold butter. Remove ½ cup (65g) of the crumb mixture and set aside.

Beat the eggs until frothy and lemon colored, then add the buttermilk. Combine this with the crumb mixture and pour into the prepared pie shell. Scatter the reserved crumbs over the top. Combine the tablespoon of sugar and the cinnamon and scatter this evenly as topping over the pie. Bake for 45 minutes in the preheated oven or until the pie has fully risen and set like cake in the center. Cool on a rack.

Raspberry Thick Milk Pie
Dickemillichboi mit Himbeere

Our recipe comes courtesy of Marian Shelly Olcott (born 1919) who grew up on a dairy farm near Fountainville, Bucks County, Pennsylvania (about 10 miles north of Doylestown). In the days before refrigeration, the family always experienced an over-abundance of clabbered milk, so during hot weather they relied heavily on traditional fruit custards. Any type of berries or other small fruits can be substituted, even herbs like peppermint or lemon thyme.

Yield: Serves 8 to 10

One 9-inch (23cm) prepared pie shell of short crust
** (page 112)**
1 pound (500g) fresh raspberries
2 large eggs
¾ cup (180ml) sour cream or clabbered milk
½ cup (125g) sugar
2 tablespoons (30ml) rosewater

Fill the prepared pie shell with fruit. Beat the eggs until lemon colored and frothy. Add the sour cream, sugar and rosewater. Whisk until well combined, then pour over the fruit. Bake in an oven preheated to 350F (180C) for 50 to 60 minutes. If your oven bakes hot, the custard will crack or curdle, in which case reduce the heat to 325F (165C) and bake 1 hour and 20 minutes instead.

If you want to use the almond pastry crust (page 110) for this recipe, I recommend using it for small tarts and baking them at 325F (165C) for 25 to 30 minutes or until set in the middle.

Slop Tarts (Thick Milk Pies)
Dickemillich Boije

Any Pennsylvania Dutch household engaged in baking on a regular basis makes slop tarts as a matter of course. The reason is simple: there are always leftover doughs and pie fillings, thus practical housewives transform the over-plus into lunchbox snacks for school children or convenient treats for morning coffee. Any size, any shape, slop tarts are so basic and easy to make that I would be remiss to leave them out of this book, in spite of their peculiar name.

One school of thought argues that the term slop tart derives from *schlappich* (sloppy), since the tarts are literally thrown together from leftovers. Other informants have suggested the name has to do with appearance: the tarts never bake in a neat and tidy manner; they are messy-but-good, given to overflowing, puffing up in the oven, and then deflating all over the crust. In short, there is no certain rule for making picture-perfect slop tarts, as my photo can attest. All the same, they make delightful snacks once you bite into them. And frankly, I think the best ones are the smallest, the little guys baked in tartlet tins.

Finally, something about the key ingredient: thick milk. The traditional ingredient in slop tarts was clabbered milk, raw milk that thickens into a junket-like consistency (similar to *Quark* in Germany). Since raw milk is no longer readily available, real clabber is not easy to come by, even though it was once considered a health food. In the age before refrigeration on Pennsylvania farms (pre-1920s), thick milk or clabber was created with "Sunday morning milk." Cows milked on Saturday night or Sunday produced milk that could not be sold until Monday; thus it soured into clabber. The

GERMANSVILLE HOTEL. GERMANSVILLE PA.

overabundance of Sunday morning milk provided country cooks with a challenge they transformed into a clever range of sour milk recipes. Unless you have your own certified raw milk clabber, use yoghurt as a substitute. The recipe that follows dates from 1916 and comes from the former Germansville Hotel in Germansville, Pennsylvania.

Yield: one 9-inch (23cm) pie or about 24 tartlets

1 large egg, separated
1 cup (250ml) thick milk, quark, or plain organic yoghurt
1 cup (175g) light brown sugar
3 tablespoons all-purpose flour or potato starch
2 teaspoons baking powder
½ teaspoon freshly grated nutmeg
½ teaspoon ground cloves

Preheat the oven to 350F (180C). Line a pie tin with dough and set aside. Beat the egg yolk until frothy, and combine with the thick milk. Add the sugar and beat until the sugar is fully dissolved. Sift together the flour, baking powder, and spices, then add this to the batter. Beat the egg white until stiff and forming peaks and fold this into the pie filling. Pour this into a prepared 9-inch (23cm) pie shell and bake in the preheated oven for approximately 40 to 45 minutes or until fully risen and set in the center. Remove from the oven and cool on a rack. The pie will deflate as it cools. This is normal.

Alternate Suggestion: Since these pies were often made for children, they are quite attractive when baked in 6-inch (15cm) tart shells or even small tartlet tins. This recipe will yield four 6-inch (15cm) tarts. They should be baked for 25 to 30 minutes. Smaller tarts will require about 20 to 25 minutes for baking. For a recommended crust, refer to Uncle Penny's Tender Pie Crust in the sidebar on page 153.

Sweet Corn and Pawpaw Pudding

SIX

SCHLUPPERS AND PUDDINGS

Die Schlupper un die Budding

The recipes in our final chapter represent a mélange of delicious, easy-to-make traditional desserts still enjoyed throughout the Dutch Country. Many types of puddings, especially the Victorian steamed puddings prepared in molds, have fallen out of fashion in favor of lighter fare – although many Amish families still enjoy them. The lightest of the light are the Cumberland Valley clafty puddings, which are essentially sponge cakes baked on top of stewed fruit. In the opposite direction (heading toward fulsome), we have the *Schlupper*, which resembles a soufflé when hot from the oven, but then assumes a dense stick-to-the-ribs texture if allowed to cool and stand overnight. The *Schlupper* is one of the most ubiquitous of all the traditional types of puddings still prepared in our regional farmhouse kitchens, and it is known by a variety of local names.

Schlupper is old-fashioned dialect for baked puddings made with bread, particularly stale bread or with day-old *Backgnepp* (see Anise Dumplings for Festive Occasions, page 7). The word came into Pennsylvania Dutch from Swabian, a term English-speaking Pennsylvanians corrupted into slump. Thus, in our part of the U.S. a slump pudding became the vernacular word for any sort of deep-dish bread pudding. This term also traveled down the Appalachians into the Upper South, where slumps of all kinds are still part of traditional fare.

The deep baking dish in question, among the Dutch at least, was a utensil called a *Rutscher*, illustrated on page 166. The most common ones were made of pottery, and several examples of local manufacture have come to light in Moravian archaeological sites in Pennsylvania as well as North Carolina. A typical *Rutscher* makes enough to feed at least 10 people, so it was supremely economical in farmhouse cookery, especially since the practical purpose of the *Schlupper* was to find creative ways for using up leftovers or an over-plus of fruit.

Blackberry or Brambleberry Clafty

Brombiere Glaafdi

In the western reaches of the Dutch Country, where narrow valleys finger their way into the Allegheny Highlands, the Pennsylvania Dutch found themselves settling side by side with the Scotch-Irish. The two communities did not always live in harmony, but over time, as they began to intermarry, their food-ways mingled. As a result, we find fascinating hybrids like this one, which hails from northern Bedford County, courtesy of the Hoenstein family.

Another version of clafty pudding from an 1881 Cumberland Valley cookbook (published in *Pennsylvania Dutch Country Cooking*) suggests that such cross-cultural fertilization was once common in central Pennsylvania – a cultural exchange that piqued the interest of American linguist H. L. Mencken. The puzzle lay in the Dutch name *Glaafdi*, which we have now identified as a term borrowed from Scotch-Irish dialect: *claffie*, meaning disordered, disheveled, or more humorously, a loose woman – perhaps a hidden pun in the name?

According to the late folklife scholar Don Yoder, in Centre County this same word with the same meaning was pronounced claddie and is still in use among farming families in that area. The origin of the odd hybrid name derives from the fact that once the pudding was baked, it was turned out upside down into a bowl or on a platter so that the gooey fruit on the bottom ended up on top. Thus it did look disheveled, yet when served in a bowl of cream or milk (or even better, with ice cream) and the addition of a little more stewed fruit as sauce, who would think to complain about the refreshing and intense flavors of wild-harvest berries plucked from the branch, wet with morning dew?

Yield: Serves 8

Fine breadcrumbs or cracker crumbs for dusting
3 cups (225g) fresh blackberries, capped and cleaned
1 cup (125g) fresh black currants or shadbush berries (see note)
1 tablespoon shredded lemon zest
¼ cup (65ml) crème de cassis
½ cup (125g) sugar
1 cup (125g) cake flour
2 teaspoons baking powder
1 teaspoon ground cinnamon
1 teaspoon ground cloves
4 large eggs
1 cup (250g) vanilla sugar
Confectioners (10-X) sugar

Preheat the oven to 375F (190C). Grease a 10½-inch (27cm) porcelain baking dish or six 6-inch (15cm) individual ceramic baking dishes (be certain the baking dishes are at least 2 inches (5cm) deep). Dust liberally with cracker crumbs or fine breadcrumbs and set aside.

In a large work bowl, combine 2 cups (150g) of blackberries, all the currants, the lemon zest, cassis and sugar. Puree the remaining blackberries and add this to the fruit mixture. Pour the fruit into the baking dish or dishes and spread evenly.

Sift together the flour, baking powder, cinnamon and cloves in a large work bowl. Using an electric mixer, beat the eggs until lemon colored and frothy, then gradually beat in the sugar until the mixture is light and creamy (about 5 to 8 minutes). Gradually sift in the dry ingredients until they form a thick, ropey batter. Pour this over the fruit and bake in the preheated oven for 30 to 35 minutes or until the batter is fully risen and the center is set. For the smaller baking dishes allow about 25 minutes. Cool on a rack and turn out on a platter (old style), or simply dust with confectioner's sugar and garnish with fruit. Serve at room temperature.

Observation: If you do not have black currants, just substitute another cup of blackberries, or use huckleberries if you want to heighten the flavor.

Boskie Boys
Bosckibuwe

Sometimes ornamented with little coils of dough or tiny pretzels, Boskie Boys are baked ball-like dumplings that were made for Christmas, New Year's or for other special occasions. Like clafty pudding, their name came into Pennsylvania Dutch from the Scotch-Irish. In Scottish dialect *boskie* means drunken, and that is precisely what these dumplings are: soaked and aged a few weeks in rum, wine or whiskey. In the eastern parts of the Dutch Country, in the area around Bethlehem, Pennsylvania, for example, Boskie Boys are known as Bowlers or Bowler Boys *(Bohler Buwe)*, since they were said to resemble the balls used by the "wee folk" *(die gleene Leit)* when they played ten pins. For good luck, toss a Boskie Boy over the house at twelve on New Year's Eve – and don't forget to make a wish when you do it.

Special equipment: For this recipe you will need fritter pans with half-spherical cups (see photograph).

Yield: approximately 72

1 tablespoon dry active yeast
2 cups (500ml) lukewarm milk (98F/37C)
1 cup (250ml) warm potato water (98F/37C)
8 cups (1 kilo) bread flour
4 large eggs
1 cup (250g) sugar
8 tablespoons (125g) unsalted butter (soft)
1 teaspoon salt
1 tablespoon freshly grated nutmeg
1 egg yolk
2 tablespoons (30ml) whole milk

Proof the yeast in the warm milk. Once the yeast is foaming, combine it with the warm potato water. Put 3 cups (375g) of bread flour in a deep work bowl and make a valley in the center. Add the yeast mixture and stir to form a thin batter. Cover and let this rise in a warm place until it forms bubbles on top (at least 2 to 3 hours). Once it is covered with bubbles, in a separate bowl beat the eggs until lemon colored and frothy. Add the sugar and beat until creamy, then add the butter, salt and nutmeg. Pour this into the batter and stir to fully combine the ingredients. Gradually sift in the 5 cups (625g) of flour, only enough to make soft dough that no longer sticks to the fingers.

Cover and let this rise until double in bulk (1 to 2 hours, depending on the weather). Knock down and knead until spongy, dusting the hands and work surface with flour as you knead. Mold the dough into 1-ounce (30g) balls and set them in greased fritter pans with small round cups. If you prefer, reserve one or two balls of dough and make small coils of dough or tiny pretzels; moisten the undersides with egg white and "glue" them to the top of each ball. Brush the ornaments with 1 egg yolk whisked into 2 tablespoons of milk. Preheat the oven to 375F (190C). While the oven is heating, cover the dough and let it recover for 25 minutes. Bake in the preheated oven for 20 to 25 minutes or until the balls tap done. Cool on a rack.

Once cool, transfer the dumplings to a non-reactive container, dip cheesecloth in rum, whisky, brandy or wine of your choice and wrap the dumplings in the cloth. Sprinkle additional rum over the top, seal with a tight-fitting lid and let the dumplings age for 2 to 3 weeks in a cool place before serving. Check from time to time in case additional rum is required – the amount is a matter of personal taste.

Alternate Suggestion: If you prefer not to age the dumplings in alcohol, you can glaze them as soon as they arrive hot from the oven. For the glaze: while they are baking, combine:

1 cup (250ml) water
1 cup (250g) sugar
1 teaspoon cinnamon

Boil these ingredients in a saucepan over a high heat until they form thick syrup. As soon as the Boskie Boys come from the oven, brush them with this syrup. As they cool, the syrup will form a shiny glaze.

Chocolate Gribble Pudding
Semmeda Budding

Gribble comes from *Grimmel*, a dialect word for large crumbs. Gribble pudding is a rich custardy dish tracing back to the Middle Ages. It resembles rice pudding, except that it is made with pasta chopped to the consistency of oatmeal. Buckwheat gribble, a key ingredient in this recipe, was made with buckwheat flour and water and resembles Grape-Nuts in texture, thus giving the dish its characteristic texture. Historically, buckwheat gribble and gribble made from rye flour were often mixed with the flour of black spelt; this type of gribble went by the name of *Semmeda* in Pennsylfaanisch to distinguish it from pasta-based gribble. Regardless, the pudding was labor intensive, and since it contained eggs and cream, gribble pudding was originally reserved for special occasions or, in the Dutch Country, as a Sunday dinner dish in country hotels.

Clara Lutz Bowman (1864-1957), longtime cook at the legendary Black Horse Hotel in Reinholds, Pennsylvania, reinvented the dish in the 1920s and put Chocolate Gribble Pudding on her menu to attract clientele from cities in the area. She enjoyed an enthusiastic following among Pennsylvania Dutch gourmets, including Frederick Klees, Cornelius Weygandt and J. George Frederick, who sometimes mentioned her in their books.

You can serve this pudding in a soufflé dish or, as was the common custom among country cooks, in a pre-baked pie shell. This makes it easier to serve as "pudding-pie" – the ideal crust is Uncle Penny's (recipe opposite). However, if you choose to use the almond crust (page 110) or the egg yolk crust (page 139), the end result will be equally sinfully delicious.

Yield: Two 9-inch (23cm) pies serving 12 to 16

¼ cup (30g) baking cocoa
½ cup (125g) light brown sugar
½ teaspoon salt
2 teaspoons ground cassia
¼ teaspoon ground cloves
½ teaspoon ground mace
1 teaspoon grated zest of orange (optional)
1½ cups (375ml) half-and-half
½ cup (125ml) strong black coffee
2 tablespoons (30g) unsalted butter
3 eggs, separated
1 cup (125g) buckwheat gribble (see Gribble Iron in glossary, on page 164) or substitute Grape-Nuts
Two pre-baked 9-inch (23cm) pie shells (½ batch of Uncle Penny's Tender Pie Crust, recipe opposite)
4 tablespoons (60g) caster sugar (bar sugar)
Shreds of bitter chocolate

Stovetop Method: Combine the chocolate, sugar, salt and spices and set aside. Take a deep saucepan and add the half-and-half, coffee and butter. Stew over a low heat until the butter is melted, then add the chocolate and spice mixture. Whisk continuously until thick and creamy. Beat the yolks until frothy and lemon colored, and fold them into the batter; whisk vigorously until they thicken. Remove from the heat and let the filling mixture cool, then add the gribble or Grape-Nuts. Pour this into the pre-baked 9-inch (23cm) pie shells or the equivalent size well-greased soufflé dishes until they are 2/3 full.

Preheat the oven to 275F (135C). Beat the egg whites until stiff and forming peaks, sweetening them with 2 tablespoons (30g) of caster sugar (bar sugar) and whisking vigorously until glossy. Gradually add 2 tablespoons (30g) more caster sugar. Spread the meringue over the top of the filling, dust with additional caster sugar and bake in the preheated oven for 10 to 15 minutes or until the meringue begins to turn golden brown on top. When cool, garnish with shreds of bitter chocolate.

Uncle Penny's Tender Pie Crust

Uncle Penny, as he is popularly known, is Francis Jacob, a sparkling-eyed old gentleman with the kind and generous spirit of Santa Claus. Uncle Penny resides in Macungie but grew up at Fruitville, a tiny crossroads near East Greenville, Pennsylvania – old maps will prove its existence. Uncle Penny is well known locally for his out-of-this-world pies, especially cherry pies with fruit harvested from his own trees. Francis donates most of his legendary pies to charitable causes, and lucky they are, because the pies bring phenomenal prices. Uncle Penny developed this crust recipe as an improvement on one created by his mother, Annie Brey Jacob (1883-1959), and it has been a closely held family treasure until he recently shared it with me.

Yield: Sufficient dough for four 9-inch (23cm) bottom crusts

3½ cups (445g) all-purpose flour
½ teaspoon salt
2 teaspoons baking powder
2 tablespoons (30g) sugar
1½ cup (375g) unsalted butter
6 egg yolks
2 tablespoons (30ml) spring water or
   bottled water

Sift together the flour, salt, baking powder and sugar. Work this into crumbs with the butter. Beat the egg yolks until lemon colored and frothy, and combine with the water. Make a valley in the center of the dry ingredients and stir with a horn fork until it forms soft, sticky crumbs. Divide the crumbs into four equal parts and form into balls. Place one ball in the center of a 9-inch (23cm) pie pan and press it with the fingers until it fills the pan. Form an edge along the rim by pinching the dough. Prick with a fork and bake in an oven preheated to 350F (180C) for 15 minutes. Allow the crust to cool before adding a pre-cooked filling.

Watch Point and Observation: Baking weights (traditionally a linen bag filled with old beans) can be placed in the empty shell to keep it from warping or shrinking while it bakes. Keep unused crumbs or portions of dough in the refrigerator until needed. Otherwise, make the additional pie shells and freeze them unbaked for later use.

Poprobin Pudding
Gnepplin Pudding

The Germans call them *Spätzle*, the Pennsylvania Dutch call them *Gnepplin* ("mini-dumplings"), and in the nineteenth century, the English-speaking neighbors of the Dutch called them poprobins. The term poprobin is a clumsy translation of *Spätzle*, adjusted to the popular misconception that the name of the German dumpling refers to a small bird or sparrow. In fact, *Spätzle* is the medieval German-ized equivalent of Latin *spatullus*, the tiny spatula originally used the make these Ancient Roman-era dumplings. Just to add to the linguistic confusion, the term poprobin also refers to rivvels, at least in the Anglo-dialect of Southeastern Pennsylvania. Thus, depending on the historical context, a poprobin was just some type of doughy dumpling regardless of size or shape. The Dutch, however, knew the difference.

Linguistics aside, poprobins were at one time fairly common in southeastern Pennsylvania cookery and remained on country tables well into the 1950s. The need to find an appropriate use for leftover dumplings gave rise to pudding recipes like this one, which was dictated orally to the late folklife scholar Alfred L. Shoemaker by Ida Fry (1865-1960) of Fry's Mill, in Lancaster County. By coincidence, this is the same garrulous and generous Mrs. Fry who shared her popular shoofly pie recipe with my grandmother.

Aside from oral tradition, poprobin pudding is often found in regional manuscript cookbooks, because it could serve both as a practical supper dish and as breakfast fare eaten with Sunday morning milk – or even better, sliced and grilled or lightly browned in a skillet and drizzled with honey. Like the *Schlupper* in the recipe following this, poprobin pudding is best when served hot from the oven. While the recipe provided here is more or less basic, you can add chopped fruit, dried cherries, sausage or mushrooms (leave out the sugar and cream), or chicken and corn (eliminate the sugar, add sweet basil); the variations are almost infinite. Just reduce the amount of dumplings equal to the weight of added fruit or meat.

Yield: Serves 8 to 10

Fine breadcrumbs or cracker meal
5½ cups (625g) pre-made packaged *Spätzle*
(or make your own)
3 eggs, separated
1½ cups (375ml) whole milk
½ cup (125g) light brown sugar
1 teaspoon ground cinnamon
½ teaspoon freshly grated nutmeg
Grated zest of ½ lemon
2 teaspoons anise (optional)
½ cup (125ml) cream or half-and-half

Grease a 2-quart (2 liter) loaf pan and dust liberally with breadcrumbs. Set aside.

Bring 3 quarts (3 liters) of lightly salted water to a full boil in a large stewing pan. Reduce the heat to a simmer and add the *Spätzle*; cook uncovered for 20 to 25 minutes or until the dumplings float and are tender when tested with a fork. Strain and discard the cooking water. Place the dumplings in a deep work bowl.

Preheat the oven to 400F (200C). Beat the egg yolks until lemon colored, and add the milk, sugar, spices and lemon. Whisk until the sugar is dissolved, then pour this over the cooked dumplings. Beat the egg whites until stiff and forming peaks, then fold into the dumpling mixture. Pour this into a well-greased loaf pan and pat smooth with the back of a large spoon or wooden paddle. Distribute the cream evenly over the surface of the dumpling mixture and bake uncovered for 10 minutes on the middle rack in the oven preheated to 400F (200C). Reduce the baking temperature

to 350F (180C) and continue baking for 25 to 30 minutes or until the pudding is set in the center and golden brown on top. Send to the table while hot and serve sliced with ice cream or stewed fruit.

Observation: If there is pudding left over, it can be turned out of the pan and refrigerated overnight on a platter or glass dish. Slice like polenta and brown lightly in a well-buttered skillet. Serve hot like pancakes with honey or maple syrup.

Sour Cherry Schlupper
Saurkarrsche Schlupper

This recipe will provide you with the basic proportions for creating an authentic Pennsylvania Dutch *Schlupper*. While cherries may be the national fruit of the Pennsylvania Dutch, with sour cherries taking place of honor when they are in season during the final weeks of June, any small fruits will work in this recipe. Raspberries are a natural, yet if you want a truly sensational mixture, try red currants, sour cherries and raspberries together. For something different, mix rhubarb and gooseberries; and instead of lemon zest, use orange zest.

The secret to a perfect *Schlupper* lies in the bread: always use the best quality sourdough loaf. Commercial white bread will only degrade into insipid mush; you must demand real bread made from non-GMO organic grains. The most traditionally correct choice would be sourdough spelt bread, but bread made from other ancient health grains will work just as well.

Yield: 8 to 10 servings (minimum)

1 pound (500g) sourdough bread trimmed of crusts
4 tablespoons (60g) unsalted butter, soft or
semi-melted
2 cups (400g) pitted sour cherries, coarsely
chopped (save the juice!)
1/3 cup (90g) light brown sugar
Grated zest of 1/2 lemon
2 teaspoons freshly grated nutmeg
4 large eggs
2 1/2 cups (625ml) whole milk
1/2 cup (125ml) sour cherry juice
2 tablespoons (30ml) vanilla flavoring

Preheat the oven to 325F (165C). Grease a 4-inch (10cm) deep 3-quart (3 liter) Le Creuset stewing pan or an earthenware baking dish like the traditional Rutscher shown here. Slice the sourdough bread as thin as possible. Brush half the slices with 3 table-spoons (45g) of semi-melted butter. Coarsely chop or dice the remaining bread and set aside. Combine the cherries, sugar, lemon and nutmeg in a small work bowl. Make a layer of buttered bread on the bottom of the well-greased baking dish and cover this with 1/2 cup (100g) of the chopped cherries. Make another layer of buttered bread and cover this with the remaining cherries. Cover the cherries with the chopped bread.

Beat the eggs until frothy and lemon colored, then add the milk, cherry juice and vanilla. Drizzle this over the bread and set aside to allow the bread to absorb most of the liquid (about 5 minutes). Dot the top with the remaining butter and bake in the preheated oven for approximately 1 hour or until the top begins to turn golden. Serve hot from the oven or at room tem-perature with slightly sweetened whipped cream.

Sweet Corn and Pawpaw Pudding
Siesskann un Baaboi Budding

The appearance of pawpaws in the Dutch Country in late August through September and even into early October is always a special event. They flood the local farm markets, and then almost as suddenly, disappear. Pawpaws have always been part of our regional food culture. At one time, impenetrable thickets of the trees grew in the rich bottom lands along local rivers and streams. Development has mostly pushed pawpaws out of their native habitats, but many market farmers have planted them in impressive numbers, so finding pawpaws is only a matter of making the right connections.

It was on a brilliant, sunny Labor Day weekend in 1989 when I first connected with the recipe that follows. The pudding was featured at a picnic on the grounds of a Church of the Brethren meeting house in Franklin County. It was being served as a side dish with steamed crabs and fresh clams. The combination is classic and the unique flavor of the pudding is unforgettable. However, a word of caution: a small minority of people is allergic to cooked pawpaws, so if you have never eaten pawpaws, start off your experiment prudently with a trial tasting.

Yield: Serves 8 to 10

4 cups (1 liter) fresh sweet corn
3 cups (750ml) pawpaw puree
3 eggs, yolks and whites separated
1 cup (250ml) milk
4 tablespoons (60ml) melted unsalted butter
½ teaspoon salt
2 tablespoons (30g) light brown sugar or to taste

Preheat oven to 350F (180C). Grease a 9 by 12 by 2-inch (23 by 30 by 5cm) porcelain baking dish or a large earthenware *Schales* pan. Grate and puree the corn in a food processor and set aside. Puree the pawpaw in the food processor and add the egg yolks, pulsing the mixture until thick and creamy. Then add the milk, melted butter and salt. Pour into work bowl and fold in the corn. Beat the egg whites until they form stiff peaks, and fold them into the batter. Adjust sweetness with the sugar, more or less depending on the ripeness of the pawpaws. Pour the batter into the prepared baking dish and bake 45 minutes or until fully risen and set in the center. Serve at room temperature.

York County Peppermint Pudding
Yarrich Kaundi Pefferminz Budding

Years ago, peppermint puddings and peppermint pies used to turn up regularly in the York and Adams County farmers markets, especially around Easter. These custardy milk puddings, very similar in texture to soufflés, are particularly refreshing when served chilled and flavored generously with peppermint. The secret to their flavor is black peppermint, a popular variety among the Pennsylvania Dutch – much sought after for its intense taste, which is also well suited for peppermint tea and anything else calling for this herb.

I have included a picture of black peppermint (below) because it is distinctive: the stems are black and the leaves dark black-green. If you can get a patch of it started in your garden, you will be well supplied throughout the growing season with an abundance of fragrant cuttings for all sorts of creative recipes – even the flowers can be infused in vinegar and used for flavoring in salads.

Yield: 4 to 6 individual servings, depending on the size of the baking cups.

Fine breadcrumbs
½ cup (35g) freshly minced peppermint leaves
4 large eggs, yolks and whites separated
1½ cups (375ml) organic yoghurt or sour cream
½ cup (125g) caster sugar
 (also called superfine sugar)
2 tablespoons potato starch
8 drops peppermint oil (optional)

Preheat the oven to 325F (165C). Grease your baking cups and dust them liberally with fine bread crumbs, then scatter the minced leaves over the bottom of each cup, making certain that the peppermint is distributed evenly. Beat the egg yolks until frothy and lemon colored, then combine this with the yogurt. Sift together the sugar and potato starch, then sift this into the egg mixture. Once these ingredients are well blended, add the optional peppermint oil to taste. Beat the egg whites until they form stiff peaks, then fold them into the peppermint batter. Fill the prepared baking cups with the batter and set the cups in a glass casserole dish. Fill the dish with hot water so that it reaches over half way up the sides of the baking cups. Bake in the preheated oven for 50 to 60 minutes or until fully set in the center. Carefully remove the cups from the water and cool on a rack. Serve slightly chilled with a garnish of peppermint leaves.

Watch Point: Due to its delicate texture, this pudding is best baked in small earthenware or china cups. Pyrex cups tend to bake hot, so baking time may be shorter.

St. Gertrude's Datsch

An Illustrated Glossary of Pennsylvania Dutch Baking Terms and Tools

ARRACK. A distillate flavored with anise. Used since the Middle Ages to flavor pastries, the most authentic old-style arracks sold in the U.S. come from Lebanon. Italians make a similar although slightly sweeter product called Anisette.

BAKING WAFERS *(Oblaten)*. Small discs of starch and egg white placed under cookies to prevent their sticking to the baking sheet. The wafers are completely edible and are normally baked under *Lebkuchen* or macaroons.

BLUE FENUGREEK *(Trigonella caerulea)*. This fragrant herb is first cousin to true fenugreek and was once grown extensively by the Pennsylvania Dutch to flavor various types of cheese, especially grating cheeses made from goat's milk, hence its Dutchname *Schabziegergraut*. The leaves were the part used in cheese; the seeds were used in baking. The ripe seeds are milder than true fenugreek and are produced in abundance.

BREAD STAMP *(Brodstempel)*. These are carved wooden molds with geometric patterns for pressing into the upper crust of breads or rolls. The designs are often symbolic and associated with pre-Christian symbolism. The stamp shown in the photograph was a common design in Lebanon County. An original bread stamp with this motif has been preserved in the collection of the late Robert R. Hellman of Lebanon, Pennsylvania.

DOUGH BREAK

(Deegbrech). A long wooden bat-like utensil used for beating dough in order to break down gluten and tenderize the dough. This was once a common procedure for making biscuits and gingerbread so that they achieved a distinctive soft, puffy texture – a similar concept for making Maryland beaten biscuits. While this procedure may

seem like a tedious lost art, the organic flours of the times and the artisanal way in which they were hand-processed produced baked goods of a quality and texture unequal to the chemically leavened counterparts of the present age.

DUMPLING BOARD *(Gnepplinbret).*

This is a flat board resembling a cutting board with a handle on one end. The board was normally held over a kettle of boiling water. A lump of dough was then placed on it and chopped with a knife or dumpling "spade," a traditional utensil for making Pennsylvania Dutch *Gnepplin* and Swabian **Spätzle**. These "spades" came in many different sizes, two of which are illustrated here.

FLOUR AND CORNMEAL.

In all of our recipes we have used locally grown, non-GMO organic flours and cornmeals produced by old-style Pennsylvania grist mills. A list of those mills may be found in the source guide on page 174. For clarification, when we call for cake flour, we are referring to a soft spring wheat flour used exclusively for cakes, as opposed to pastry flour, which is designed for cookies, pie crusts and similar desserts. Bread flour and all-purpose flour are the other two types used in this book. For best results use the type of flour that we specify in each recipe. If you want to use flours from locally-grown grains, as we do in Pennsylvania, then refer to the list of mills on page 174.

GINGERBREAD CUTTER.

A type of rolling pin with evenly spaced sharp, metal disc-shaped blades used for cutting gingerbreads and other types of dough into squares or rectangles. They are also called *Nudelschnitter*, since they were used to make *Schnitt-Nudle*, "snip noodles" (diamond-shaped dumplings), and even pot pies (squares of noodle dough). These handmade utensils were in widespread use before local bakeries became mechanized.

GRIBBLE IRON *(Gribbeleise).*

A miniature spatula used with the dumpling board to make dumplings or otherwise employed in chopping buckwheat dough into tiny bits in a skillet or frying pan. These distinctive miniature spatulas were not produced commercially, rather by local whitesmiths or

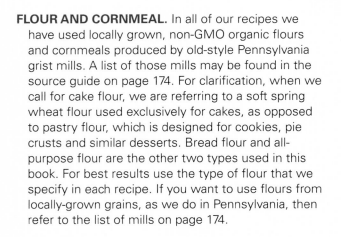

ironsmiths – hence they are now considered valuable heirlooms. The tiny bits of dough they made were known colloquially as gribble. The photo shows both gribble and the 1830s iron that produced it.

HAIL SUGAR *(Hagelzucker)*. This is special type of decorative sugar that resembles the coarse salt on pretzels. For this reason it is used on sugar pretzels, but also on cookies where you might want them to appear frosted with snow. Hail sugar is sold commercially online, usually under its German name. The image shows three types of hail sugar, the most coarse being "crystal sugar" – frozen "ice" meant to sparkle on pastries fresh from the oven.

MESSEPICK. A rare Pennsylvania Dutch term not easily translated into English. It is a humorous Civil War expression for a spread of dishes in the officers' canteen: an oddball assortment of foods brought together in a hurry on the battlefield. In practice it became a type of buffet where everything from soups to desserts was laid out together for grazing – the Pennsylvania Dutch equivalent of Spanish tapas or Greek mezze.

NEW YEAR'S CAKE *(Neijohrs Kuche)*. These pictorial cookies became popular during the late eighteenth century in connection with New Year's open house entertainments in New York and continued in popularity throughout the nineteenth century. The cakes originated in the Hudson Valley, but as the custom moved into other areas of the East, they were adjusted to local practice and iconography. For example, the best New York molds were carved by John Conger from Connecticut, and images on Baltimore New Year's Cakes reflected Baltimore themes associated with local events. Often made of mahogany, the overall style and large size of the molds are distinct from Springerle and gingerbread molds and are peculiarly American in style and concept. On that note, Pennsylvania Dutch New Year's Cake molds tend to be patriotic, with images drawn from local oral culture. All the same, New Year's Cakes were not a homegrown custom, so the motifs decorating them are not related to local folk iconography, like the pretzel, Antler Cookies, and Fish Pie.

NOODLE ROLLING PIN *(NUDELHOLZ)*. A type of rolling pin with ridges that cut noodle dough into small thin strips or threads. The rollers were highly prized by Pennsylvania Dutch cooks because they eliminated the need to hand-cut the noodles with a sharp knife, thus saving time in the kitchen. These rolling pins were also used to cut pie crusts into spaghetti-like strips for making "nest pies," top crusts resembling bird nests.

PASTRY WHEEL
(Drollrad). A tool for both cutting and ornamenting pastry crusts or for cutting out noodle dough. Old-style and antique pastry wheels are available online from eBay.com.

PICOSO SUGAR *(Scharfzucker).* A mixture of sugar, hot chili powder and cassia. A traditional spice mixture on certain types of fat cakes and fritters.

ROLLING PIN *(Drollholz).* There are several words in Pennsylvania Dutch for rolling pins, but this term seems to be the one most in common use and related etymologically to other pastry tools. See, for example, pastry wheel. There were wooden rolling pins (the most common sort), as well as glass, marble, and slate pins that are now quite rare as collectors' items. Both the traditional gray Chester County marble and the Lehigh County slate rolling pins work extraordinarily well in recipes where cold rolling pins are called for, the Stollen recipe on page 25, for one.

RUTSCHER. A traditional baking pan with a handle on one end and a spout on the other. Some also came with matching lids. Several types of Pennsylvania Dutch desserts were prepared in a Rutscher, including the baked pudding known as *Schlupper.* Any earthenware deep-dish casserole pan or a German *Römertopf* can be used as substitutes.

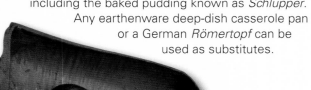

SAFFRON *(Safferich).*
Crocus sativus is used extensively in Pennsylvania Dutch festive cookery and the best sorts are locally grown. Saffron has been raised since the 1730s in Pennsylvania, the heirloom varieties being much more flavorful than imported Spanish saffron. All saffron used in this book was grown in the author's kitchen garden

and descends from an heirloom strain still grown in the area around Schaefferstown, Pennsylvania. In the Dutch Country, Schaefferstown saffron is considered the best of the best.

SAUCER PIE *(Schissel Boi).* The Pennsylvania Dutch equivalent of pasties or popovers, these pies are essentially the same as Half-Moon Pies, except that they are generally larger in size and baked individually on a pie dish as opposed to Half-Moon Pies baked on cookie sheets. There are two basic types: savory for meats and vegetables and made with lard-based yeast-raised crust, and sweet for fruits and nuts made with butter-based yeast crust. They are also called *Lappkuche* ("fold-over pies"). Their special shape was achieved by folding the dough over the contents and then baking them in shallow, concave earthenware dishes or saucers. Several Pennsylvania potteries still make this type of ceramics.

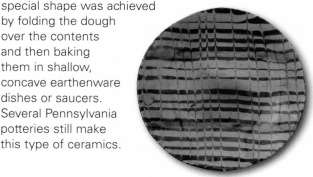

SCHALES PAN. In many recipes we refer to a specific type of Pennsylvania Dutch baking dish known as a *Schales*. The name derives from Middle High German *Schalles* and is cognate with the English words shell and shallow, and means just about the same thing: a broad, shallow baking dish similar in shape to a Spanish paella pan. Many Pennsylvania Dutch own these pans but do not call them *Schales* because the spoken dialect is dying out, thus this was a term better known to our grandmothers and great-grandmothers.

The traditional pans were made of tin, earthenware and even cast iron, although the iron ones are now quite rare. The photo shows a rare 1840s cast iron *Schales* pan and a now-scarce earthenware one made in 1984 by the late folk potter Dorothy Long. If you do not have a *Schales* pan you can improvise with an 11½ to 12-inch (29 to 30cm) cake tin with outwardly sloping 1¾-inch (3cm) sides. However, the earthenware ones are the best because of the way they retain radiant heat while in the oven.

SCHNITZ. This Pennsylvania Dutch term is used commercially in Southeastern Pennsylvania for labeling any sort of sliced dried fruit. The most common form is apple schnitz, but pear, peach, quince and apricots are also dried in this same manner.

SPRINGERLE BOARD. This term refers to a cookie mold or "print" of large dimensions depicting several scenes or images that are pressed into Springerle dough. The boards usually display six, eight, twelve or as many as sixteen images, each representing one individual cookie. Most boards are carved of hardwood, but some American made ones are made of pewter or a pewter-like alloy.

TEABERRIES. Small red candies flavored with teaberry, also known as American wintergreen (*Gaultheria procumbens*). The small candy "berries" or sprinkles are used to ornament Pennsylvania Dutch pastries, or they are dissolved in milk to flavor ice cream or cake batters.

Several online companies located in Pennsylvania offer the candies via mail order. Teaberry is considered a distinctive Pennsylvania Dutch flavor and is so marketed throughout the Dutch Country.

VANILLA SUGAR. Commercially available sugar flavored with vanilla. This is often used as a garnish on cakes and cookies. You can make your own by mixing vanilla extract with sugar and drying it at a low temperature in an oven.

Bibliography

Archer, Mary, ed. *The Belgian Relief Cook Book.* Reading, Pa.: Reading Eagle Press, 1915.

Berks County Federation of Women's Clubs. *Bicentennial Cook Book.* Reading, Pa.: Berks County Federation of Women's Clubs, 1948.

Bethany Orphans' Home League of Hain's Reformed Church, Wernersville, Pa. *Tried and True Recipes.* [Reading, Pa.: The C. F. Heller Bindery,] 1927. Fourth edition.

Bischoff, Oskar. *Das Pfälzische Weihnachtsbuch.* Neustadt an der Weinstrasse: Pfälzische Verlagsanstalt, 1970.

Boehm, Fritz. *Geburtstag und Namenstag im deutschen Volksbrauch.* Berlin/Leipzig: Walter de Gruyter & Co., 1938.

Book of Recipes for Cakes, Custards, Pies, Jellies. Gettysburg, Pa.: Shields & Aughinbaugh, 1869.

Braun, Emmy. *Neues Kochbuch.* Grünstadt: J. Schäffer's Verlagsbuchhandlung, ca. 1929. Emmy Braun was the pseudonym of Luise Lichtenberger Jacob (1826-1904).

Brocke, David. *Der Kuchenbäcker.* Quedlinburg/Leipzig: Ernst'schen Buchhandlung, 1847.

Class No. 1 of Trinity Lutheran Sunday School, Mechanicsburg, Pa. *Anniversary Cook Book.* Mechanicsburg, Pa.: Privately Printed, 1952.

Crass, Eduard. *Deutsches Brauchtum im Jahreslauf.* Leipzig: Bibliographisches Institut, 1935.

Dr. Hartman's Bible Class of St. John's Reformed Church. *Cook Book,* Emma J. Hoke, ed. . Harrisburg, Pa.: Privately Printed, ca. 1925.

Dutch Pantry. *Simply Sweets: A Collection of Favorite Recipes from Our Family to Yours.* [Gettysburg, Pa.: Dutch Pantry Restaurants, ca. 1990]. Most of the recipes are from Dutch Pantry employees in the Clearfield, Pa., restaurant.

Eiselt-Lomb, Ulrike et al., eds. *Bäuerliche Küche zwischen Hohenlohe un Bauland.* Krautheim: Heimat- und Kulturverein Krautheim, 2003.

Eupel, Johann Christian. *Der vollkommene Conditor.* Weimar: Bernhard Friedrich Voigt, 1840.

Evans, Mary Elizabeth. *Mary Elizabeth's War Time Recipes.* New York: Frederick A. Stokes, 1918.

_____. *My Candy Secrets.* New York: Frederick A. Stokes, 1919.

The Franklin County Charity Benefit Cook Book. Chambersburg, Pa.: Opinion-Register Press, 1914.

Gillespie, Mrs. E. D., ed. *The National Cookery Book.* Philadelphia: Women's Centennial Executive Committee, 1876.

Graff, Monika. *Pfeffernuss und Mandelkern.* Weil der Stadt: Walter Hädecke Verlag, ca. 1995.

Hess, Elam G., ed. *800 Proved Pecan Recipes.* Manheim, Pa.: Keystone Pecan Research Laboratory, 1925.

Jung, Mathilde. *Eine Landschaft Kocht: Ein Pfälzisches Küchenbrevier.* Neustadt an der Weinstrasse: Verlag D. Meininger, 1953.

Kaspar, Hans, ed. *Lebkuchen/Pains d'Epices.* Zurich: Hans Kaspar A.G., 1946.

Klein, Georges. *Le poisson dans l'art et les traditions populairs d'Alsace.* Strasbourg: Musée Alsaciene, 1983.

Knörin, R. Christine. *Sammlung vieler Vorschriften von allerley Koch- und Backwerk für junges Frauenzimmer.* Stuttgart: Erhardischen Buchhandlung, 1813.

Kuchenmaistery. Nuremberg: Peter Wagner, 1485.

Ladies' Aid Society of St. Paul's Lutheran and Reformed Church, Adamstown, Pa. *All About Home Baking and Cooking.* Adamstown, Pa.: Ladies' Aid Society, ca. 1950.

Ladies' Aid Society of St. Paul's Reformed Church, Ravine, Pa. *Home Tried Recipes.* Tremont: West Schuylkill Press and Pine Grove Herald, 1938.

Ladies' Auxiliary of the Y.M.C.A. *Housekeeper's Guide.* Pittston, Pa.: Item Publishing, 1896.

Lingen, Helmut, ed. *Leckere Weihnachts-Bäckerei.* Cologne: Lingen Verlag, 1979.

Mannhardt, Wilhelm. *Wald- und Feldkulte.* Darmstadt: Wissenschaftliche Buchgesellschaft, 1963. 2 volumes. Reprint of the 1905 Berlin edition.

Missionary Society of St. John's Evangelical Lutheran Church, Nazareth, Pennsylvania. *Nazareth's Own Cook Book.* Nazareth: The Nazareth Item, 1951.

Missionary Society of St. Paul's Reformed Church, Bowmansville, Pa. *Household Guide and Cook Book.* Denver, Pa.: Steffy & Co., 1916.

Pelz, Henrietta. *Neues Allgemeines Schlesisches Kochbuch.* Breslau: Eduard Pelz, 1835.

Perini, Giacomo. *Der Schweizerzuckerbäcker.* Weimar: Bernhard Friedrich Voigt, 1858.

Perl, Lila. *Red-Flannel Hash and Shoo-fly Pie: American Regional Foods and Festivals.* Cleveland: World Publishing Company, 1965.

Pfluger, Elisabeth. *Solothurner Liebesbriefe: Gebäck im Jahreslauf.* Solothurn (Switzerland): Verlag Aare, 1982.

Plagemann, Catherine. *Fine Preserving,* annotated by M. F. K. Fisher. Berkeley, CA: Aris Books, 1986.

Reichard, Harry Hess. *The Christmas Poetry of the "Pennsylvania Dutch."* Allentown, PA: Schlechter's, 1941.

Shoemaker, Alfred L. *Studies on the Pennsylvania German Dialect of the Amish Community in Arthur, Illinois.* Urbana: Thesis Abstract, University of Illinois Press, 1940.

Spörlein, Margarete. *Oberrheinisches Kochbuch.* Mülhausen: Verlag von J. P. Rissler, 1852.

Stone Valley Zion Lutheran-United Church of Christ. *Time Tested Recipes.* Stone Valley, Pa., Privately Printed, 1965.

Valentin, Hans E. *Brezen, Kletzen, Dampedei.* Regensburg: Verlag Friedrich Pustet, 1978.

Vollmer, William. *The United States Cook Book.* Philadelphia: John Weik, 1859.

Vollständiges Kochbuch für die Deutsch-Amerikanische Küche. Philadelphia: Loes & Sebald, ca. 1856

Weaver, William Woys. *The Christmas Cook: Three Centuries of American Yuletide Sweets.* New York: Harper/Collins, 1990.

_____. *Pennsylvania Dutch Country Cooking.* New York: Abbeville, 1993.

_____. *As American As Shoofly Pie: The Foodlore and Fakelore of Pennsylvania Dutch Cuisine.* Philadelphia: University of Pennsylvania Press, 2013.

White, Allene. "They Made Whoopie," *Maine Sunday Telegram* (October 16, 1988).

Wiegand, Albin, ed. *Frankfurter Kochbuch.* Frankfurt: Verlag Frankfurter Kochbuch, 1951.

Winebrenner, Mary Hamilton. *Housekeepers Book.* Harrisburg, Pa. 1837-1888. Manuscript cookery book with a collection of recipe newspaper and almanac clippings. Roughwood Collection, Devon, Pa.

Women's Missionary Society, Zion Mennonite Church, Souderton, Pa. *Cook Book of Practical Recipes.* Souderton, Pa.: Goettler & Son, 1940.

INTERVIEWS

Bryan, Kerry. Philadelphia, Pa., January 11, 2014. Born 1951. Grew up in New York City in a family of Irish descent. Worked 1971-1972 as a waitress for the Dutch Pantry in Gettysburg, Pennsylvania. Discussed menus, food specialties and the types of people who patronized the restaurant.

Davis, Annabelle Teter. Zion Grove, Pa. (Columbia County), September 8, 2013. Born 1930. Grew up in a Pennsylvania Dutch household in Zion Grove. Her father, Guy Teter, was a dairyman and truck farmer. Provided a lengthy discussion and recipe for saucer pies.

Erdman, Betty Klinger. Rough and Ready, Pa., October 27, 1992. Born 1927. Grew up in Schuylkill County in the German Reformed tradition. Wife of Emery E. Erdman (1921-1983). Spoke fluent Pennsylvania Dutch. Now deceased.

Erdman, Irene Schwalm. Valley View, Pa., August 23, 2013. Born 1917. Grew up in Valley View, the daughter of a coal minor. Speaks fluent Pennsylvania Dutch. Excellent comments on home candy making, the use of teaberries and other local ingredients.

Fry, Ida. Fry's Mill, Pa. January 4, 1955. Born 1865, Ida grew up near Ephrata, Pennsylvania where her family was engaged in a nursery business. Collected lore about St. Gertrude and Gertrude's Day. Now deceased. Interviewed by Alfred L. Shoemaker, Pennsylvania Dutch Folklife Society files, Ursinus College.

Jacob, Francis. Macungie, Pa., February 26, 2013. Retired farmer and cook for the Niantic German Reformed Church. Grew up at Fruitville (near Green Lane), Montgomery County, Pa. Known to all his friends and family as Uncle Penny.

Kemp, Evelyn Miller. Leesport, Pa. August 7, 2013. Traditional cook. Grew up in a home with a single mother in Perry Township, Berks County, Pa. Speaks fluent Pennsylvania Dutch.

Klinger, Dorothy Bush. Hegins, Pa., August 24, 2013. Born 1921, grew up on a farm at the foot of Broad Mountain. Came from a home of mixed Pennsylvania Dutch and Anglo-American culinary traditions.

Kriebel, Samuel. Souderton, Pa., March 14, 2013. Retired farmer. Grew up on his ancestral farm at Mainland (near Souderton), Montgomery County, Pa. Speaks fluent Pennsylvania Dutch.

Kulp, Isaac Clarence. Pennsburg, Pa., June 13, 2005. Born 1938, grew up near Harleysville, Montgomery County, Pa. Church of the Brethren (Dunkard) folklorist and local historian. Now deceased.

Michaels, Dean. Halifax, Pa., August 23, 2013. Born 1925, grew up in Dalmatia, Pa., in a Pennsylvania Dutch village along the Susquehanna. Knowledgeable about eel fishing in the Susquehanna, at one time an active local industry.

Miller, Renee Kemp. Paoli, Pa., December 11, 2013. Born 1958, grew up in Hamburg, Pa., in a Pennsylvania Dutch household where her grandmother did much of the traditional cooking. Personal reminiscences about making Fastnachts, about Bender's Bakery and other Dutch food purveyors.

Miller, Wayne. Littlestown, Pa., June 2, 1994. Grew up on a Littlestown farm; specializes in heirloom sweet potatoes from the collection of his grandmother Bertie Missouri Miller (1883-1964).

Moore, Dennis R. Pine Grove, Pa., November 14, 2013. Grew up in Lebanon County. Retired architectural engineer. Discussed bake oven and baking traditions at the old Quentin Hotel, Quentin, Pennsylvania (near Lebanon).

Nikischer, Frank. September 25, 2013 at the Deitsch Eck, Lenhartsville, Pa. Born 1931 in Allentown, Pa. to parents of Austrian (Burgenland) descent. His sister married into the Walp family, which owned a well-known local restaurant. In 1986 he and his wife purchased the restaurant and continued the Walp culinary tradition. After the restaurant closed, he co-authored a cookbook on Walp's most popular Pennsylvania Dutch recipes.

Rhoads, Anna M. Bally, Pa., February 2, 2013. Father was trash collector in Bally, Pa. Spent her married years on a dairy farm near Niantic, Montgomery County, PA.

Schreffler, Merlin. Klingerstown, Pa., August 24, 2013. Born 1926 on the farm where he now lives. Son of truck farmers who huckstered produce in Shamokin, PA (about 10 miles away). Speaks fluent Pennsylvania Dutch.

Shade, Doris Masser. Gratz, Pa., August 23, 2013. Born 1929 in Hegins, Pa, the daughter of a well-known Hegins grocery store keeper.

Schumann, Bernard. Hegins, Pa. Born in Brooklyn, New York, and raised by his maternal grandparents, Ira Herb and Wrela Bixler, in Hegins, Pa. Grew up immersed in Pennsylvania Dutch culture and speaks fluent Pennsylvania Dutch. He is the 5th generation to live in his grandparents' house (built 1868).

Sundberg, Anita Leyser. Mullica Hill, NJ, March 25, 2013. Grew up among the Church of the Brethren on a poultry farm near Royerstown, Lebanon County, Pa.

Werner, William E. Jefferson, Pa. February 25, 1953. Born 1869 in York County, Pennsylvania where he lived as a farmer in Codorus Township. Now deceased. Interviewed by Alfred L. Shoemaker, Pennsylvania Dutch Folklife Society files, Ursinus College.

Where to Shop for Specialty Items

Amish Roll Butter
Minerva Dairy
P. O. Box 60, Minerva, OH 44657
330-868-4196

Barrel Molasses and Leaf Lard
Dietrich's Meats and Country Store
660 Old Route 22, Krumsville, PA 19534
610-756-6344
www.dietrichsmeats.com

Cheese
Birchrun Hills Farm
2573 Horseshoe Trail Road
Chester Springs, PA 19425
www.birchrunhillsfarm.com

Chestnuts and Chestnut Flour
Allen Creek Farm
P. O. Box 841, Ridgefield, WA 98642
360-887-3669
www.Chestnutsonline.com

Cooking and Baking Supplies, Bulk Natural Foods
Echo Hill Country Store
244 Dryville Road, Fleetwood, PA 19522
610-944-7358
www.echohillcountrystore.com

Kimberton Whole Foods
2140 Kimberton Road
Kimberton, PA 19442
610-935-1444
www.kimbertonwholefoods.com
Also supplies their own line of biodynamic flours
and dairy products.

Miller's Natural Foods
2888 Miller Lane, Bird-in-Hand, PA 17505
Leave Messages at 717-768-7582
Amish Owned, No email. No credit cards.
Mail Orders via UPS

Cookie Cutters and Culinary Tinware
H. O. Foose Tinsmithing Company
18 West Poplar Street, Fleetwood, PA 19522
610-944-1960
www.foosecookiecutters.com

Dried (Toasted) Sweet Corn
Cope's Toasted Sweet Corn
Hanover Foods Corp., P.O. Box 334,
Hanover, PA 17331
717-632-6000
www.johncopes.com

Flours (Stone Ground), Roasted Cornmeal, Bread Flour, Pastry Flour

The Mill at Anselma
1730 Conestoga Road, Chester Springs, PA 19425
610-827-1906
www.anselmamill.org

Arrowhead Mills
Melville, NY 11747
1-800-431-4246
www.arrowheadmills.com

Castle Valley Mill
1730 Lower State Road, Doylestown, PA 18901
215-340-3609
www.Castlevalleymill.com

Daisy Organic Flours
(Milled at the 1740 Brandt Mill, Annville, PA)
McGeary Organics, Inc., Lancaster, PA 17608
800-624-3279
www.daisyflour.com

Haldeman Mills
1234 Mountain Road, Manheim, PA 17545
717-665-2339
www.haldemanmills.com

King Arthur Flour Company
Norwich, VT 05055
1-800-827-6836
www.kingarthurflour.com

Snavely's Mill
333 Snavely Mill Road, Lititz, PA 17543
717-626-6256
www.snavelysmill.com

Frackville Pretzel Molds (sold as Soft Pretzel Molds)

Reuben E. Mast
32187 State Route 643
Fresno, OH 43824
Amish household (no phone or email)
Also available online from:
    www.cottagecraftworks.com

Honey and Honey Products

Brandywine Bee Company
Chadds Ford, PA
610-299-4784
www.brandywinebeecompany.com
This firm maintains hives in the garden belonging to the author.

Bumbleberry Farms
Somerset, PA 15501
814-279-8083
www.bumbleberryfarms.com

Maple Syrup, Maple Sugar and Maple Sugar Products

Paul Bunyan's Maple Sugar
793 Gebhart Road, Rockwood, PA 15557
814-233-6695
www.paulbunyansmaplesyrup.com

Raspberry Products

Tait Farm
179 Tait Road
Centre Hall, PA 16828
1-800-787-2716
www.taitfarmfoods.com

Sour Dough Pretzels

Ruthie's Pretzels
219 Dryville Road, Fleetwood, PA 19522
610-944-8243

Teaberry Candies and Flavored Sugars
  Echo Hill Country Store
  244 Dryville Road, Fleetwood, PA 19522
  610-944-7358
  www.echohillcountrystore.com

Traditional Redware Potters
  (Pie plates, baking ware)
  The Foltz Pottery
  225 North Peartown Road
  Reinholds, PA 17569
  717-336-2676
  www.foltzpottery.com

  Turtlecreek Pottery
  3600 Shawhan Road
  Morrow, OH 45152
  513-932-2472
  www.davidtsmith.com

  Jeff White
  Booth 161, Black Angus Antiques Mall
  Rt. 272, Adamstown, PA 19501
  717-484-4386
  www.stoudts.com

Wooden Kitchen Utensils (Hand Carved)
  Jonathan Spoons
  3716 Route 737, Kempton, PA 19529
  800-776-6853
  www.woodspoon.com

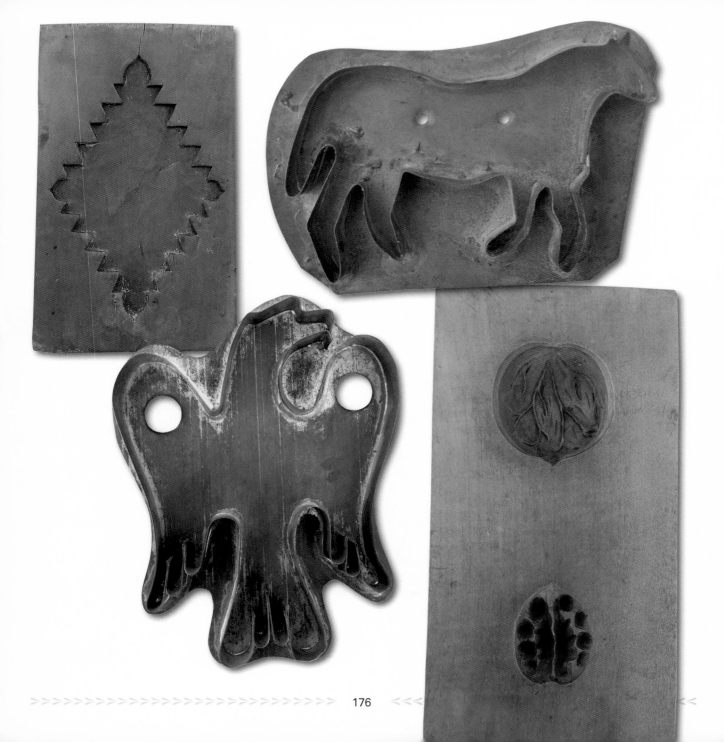

Index

Recipe List

Dutch treats await Sunday dinner in a farmhouse kitchen, Maytown, Pennsylvania, 1910.

Recipe Contributors

Grateful acknowledgment is due to the following individuals and families who so generously shared their recipes with me for this book.

Dr. Daniel Lee Backenstose: Orange Pretzels

The family of Kate Schaeffer Bennethum:
   Saffron Apeas

Mary Christine: Buttermilk Crumb Pie

Catharina Bittenbender: Almond Pastry Dough

Carrie V. Bitting: Bellylaps

Clara Lutz Bowman: Chocolate Gribble Pudding

Mrs. Leo Braucher: Apple Butter Pie

Helen Fenstermacher Breidigam: Crumb Cake

Hattie Brunner: Honey Cakes

Fannie Coble: New Year's "Boys"

Edna I. Daniel: Fish Pie

Della C. Diffenbaugh: Cinnamon Rolls or "Snails"

Betty Klinger Erdman: Rough-and-Ready Cake

Lenore K. Fitterling: Snowballs

Emma Gable: Sugar Kringles

Ivan Glick: Stollen and Strietzel

Phoebe Hanawalt: Dutch Apple Cake

Mary Hessenberger: Bishop's Bread

Anna Bertolet Hunter: Dutch Bread

Francis Jacob: Uncle Penny's Tender Pie Crust

Isaac Clarence Kulp: Nuttle Cookies

The Family of Lena H. Lebo: Filled Crumb Cake

Bertie Miller: Apple Schnitz Pie with Sweet Potatoes

Hattie Nagle: New Year's Cake

Marian Shelly Olcott: Raspberry Thick Milk Pie

Mary Peachey: Oatmeal Datsch

Gertrude Raffensburger Ibach: Cottage Cheese Tart

Carolina Levan Reber: Coffee Shoofly Cake

Edna Kline Roland: Lemon Crumb Pie

Laura Heffner Schock: Springerle Cookies

Mary Seaman Shenk: Sand Tarts

Alfred L. Shoemaker, folklife scholar (orally from
   Ida Fry): Poprobin Pudding and St. Gertrude's
   Day Datsch

Lola Hollanda Showalter: Maple Sugar Apeas

Jonas Slonaker: Mango Schnitz Pie

Ernie Risser: Snickerdoodles

Ruth Weaver: Pretzel Crust

Lydia M. Yoder: Coffee Spice Cake

Kate Zug: Whoopie Cake

Acknowledgments

*I*would like to express my thanks to the many Pennsylvania Dutch cooks who took time to sit down with me for interviews and sometimes even a few cooking demonstrations. The late Dr. Don Yoder, "father of American folklife," often accompanied me during my fieldwork, and those memories of his gentle presence will always remain with me. A large thank-you is due Patrick Donmoyer, who allowed me to use the historic farmhouse at Kutztown University as a site for some of the photography.

Drew M. McCaskey, Dan Waber and Owen Taylor, all part of the Roughwood Seed Collection team, served as my Tasting Committee. Their helpful pointers were of great use for tweaking the recipes to make each one just a little bit better.

My literary agent, Lisa Ekus, deserves a huge hug for believing in this book, and the folks at St. Lynn's Press are to be thanked for understanding its vision – especially my editor, Cathy Dees, who is a real old-school editor of the very best sort.

Lancaster trade card depicting Shoofly the boxing mule, circa 1880.

HARVEST HOME
LINGLESTOWN
CHURCH OF GOD
Oct. 31, 1926

About the Author

WILLIAM WOYS WEAVER is an internationally known food historian, the author of sixteen books and hundreds of articles on foods and foodways. His books include *A Quaker Woman's Cookbook*, *America Eats*, and *The Christmas Cook*, a 300-year history of the American Christmas. His most recent book, *As American As Shoofly Pie*, is an analysis of Pennsylvania Dutch cuisine.

He is founding president of the Historic Foodways Society of the Delaware Valley and the director of the Keystone Center for the Study of Regional Foods and Food Tourism, a non-profit academic research institute, where he teaches courses on regional American cuisine. Dr. Weaver received his doctorate in food studies at University College Dublin, Ireland, the first doctorate awarded by the University in that field of study.

His many publishing accolades include three cookbook awards from the IACP, International Association of Culinary Professionals. He was Associate Editor and Art Editor of *The Encyclopedia of Food and Culture*, which received the Dartmouth Medal from the American Library Association, the highest award in the reference book industry.

Dr. Weaver is a contributing editor to *Mother Earth News* and a regular contributor to *The Heirloom Gardener* – and, until it stopped publication, was a contributing editor to *Gourmet*. He has been the subject of articles in *Americana, Food and Wine, Food Arts, The Chicago Tribune, The New York Times* and *Country Living*.

Dr. Weaver is a board member of GMO Free Pennsylvania and the Experimental Farm Network, a grass-roots organization devoted to alternative methods of seed production. He maintains the Roughwood Seed Collection of over 4,000 heirloom food plants and lives in the 1805 Lamb Tavern, a National Register property in Devon, Pennsylvania. On the grounds of the tavern Dr. Weaver keeps a *jardin potager* in the style of the 1830s. He is an organic gardener, a life member of Seed Savers Exchange and a member of Arche Noah in Schiltern, Austria.

www.williamwoysweaver.com

OTHER BOOKS FROM ST. LYNN'S PRESS

www.stlynnspress.com

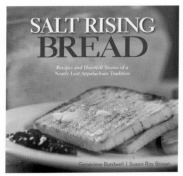

Salt Rising Bread

by Genevieve Bardwell and Susan Ray Brown

160 pages, Hardback
ISBN: 978-1-9433660-3-3

The Cocktail Hour Garden

by C.L. Fornari

160 pages, Hardback
ISBN: 978-0-9892688-0-6

Good Berry Bad Berry

by Helen Yoest

160 pages, Hardback
ISBN: 978-0-9855622-7-4

Ramps

by the Editors of St. Lynn's Press

160 pages • Hardback
ISBN: 978-0-9892688-7-5